THE NOT SO SECRET FOOTBALL AGENT

THE NOT SO SECRET FOOTBALL AGENT

BARRY SILKMAN

Reach Sport
www.reachsport.com

Reach Sport

www.reachsport.com

Copyright © Barry Silkman 2025.

The right of Barry Silkman to be identified as the owner of this work has been asserted in accordance with the Copyright, Designs and Patents Act, 1988. All Rights Reserved. No part of this publication may be reproduced, stored in a retrieval system, or transmitted in any form, or by any means, electronic, mechanical, photocopying, recording or otherwise without the prior permission in writing of the copyright holders, nor be otherwise circulated in any form of binding or cover other than in which it is published and without a similar condition being imposed on the subsequent publisher.

Written with David Clayton.

Published in Great Britain and Ireland in 2025 by Reach Sport.

www.reachsport.com
@Reach_Sport

Reach Sport is a part of Reach PLC.

Hardback ISBN: 9781914197734
eBook ISBN: 9781914197741

Cover Design: Chris Collins
Editing and production: Roy Gilfoyle, Christine Costello

Photographic acknowledgements: Getty Images, Alamy, Barry Silkman's personal collection

Every effort has been made to trace copyright.
Any oversight will be rectified in future editions.

Printed and bound by CPI Group (UK) Ltd,
Croydon, CR0 4YY.

CONTENTS

Foreword by Harry Redknapp	9
Prologue	13
Silk And Steel	17
Mum's The Word	29
The (Not So) Artful Dodgin	38
TV Times	46
Crystal Clear	60
Law Abiding Cityzen	71
The Israelite	89
The Bees' Knees	98
Spaghetti Hoops	104
The Orient Express	113
Disorientated!	131
The 'What Might Have Been' Chapter	153
Gone To The Dogs?	168
Barry Silkman: Football Agent	175
A Gent And An Agent	183
Coulda, Woulda, Shoulda	194
A Light That Never Goes Out	214
The Show Must Go On	224

For Keenia, Saul and Eran

FOREWORD

by Harry Redknapp

Me and Silky go back a long way – to his Leyton Orient days in the early 1980s in fact.

He was a skilful footballer, and I always thought that if Malcolm Allison liked you, you were good because Malcolm was a fantastic judge of players.

He had quite a few clubs and then became a football agent, almost by accident I believe!

Silky is a great judge of a player and always has been, so it made perfect sense that he became an agent, and I'd say he is the most knowledgeable football agent of the lot.

When he brings a player to your attention, you listen, and he's found many top footballers for me during my management career.

I remember he introduced me to Eyal Berkovic when

I was at West Ham United, but Spurs were in for him as well.

Eyal was an Israeli boy so we knew Spurs, with their big Jewish connection, held all the aces.

As you'll read later in the book, Silky had other ideas and after we'd spoken with Eyal, he told us that if he didn't sign for Spurs, he'd come to us.

Silky came up with an ingenious plan to make sure he didn't join Spurs, but I knew nothing of it.

Sure enough, a few hours later Eyal called to say he was joining West Ham – read how he did later in this book because it still makes me chuckle today.

He also brought me some players that I didn't rate – and went on to regret it!

He brought me Mario Melchiot and Nemanja Vidic, but for one reason or another I didn't take his advice, and both went on to have incredible spells at Chelsea and Manchester United respectively.

He still reminds me of that occasionally!

Silky is a genuinely nice bloke, and a real character.

He is great to be around, and I really enjoy his company – but I had no idea he was a singer, too!

I went to watch a night of soul stars recently in Bournemouth with people like Rose Royce, and before the show began Silky walked on to the stage in his glittery showbiz suit and I thought, 'Oh no Silky, don't embarrass yourself'.

FOREWORD

He then started singing 'Me and Mrs Jones' and he was fantastic.

He's a man of many talents, that's for sure, and it is a pleasure to be able to open his book with my recollections of him.

I guarantee you'll enjoy what you are about to read because with Silky, there really is never a dull moment!

Harry Redknapp, Sandbanks,
November 2024

PROLOGUE

"Mum, I think I've pissed myself."

This is the first memory I have of pretty much anything and it's where we'll begin this story of my life as – in no particular order – a footballer, singer, football agent and impresario.

It's been colourful, funny, joyous, and occasionally an incredibly sad journey, but that's how life is and you learn to take the happy times with the odd slug in the guts – and I've had plenty of the former and one or two of the latter in my 72 (and counting) years on this planet.

For the things I've been able to control, I wouldn't change a thing.

As for the things I couldn't control, I'd almost certainly change everything, but then, wouldn't we all given the chance? You play with the deck you've been given, make the most of it and see where it takes you, and apart from my personal family losses, I've had a riot up to this point and appreciated every single moment with those I've loved, but aren't alongside me anymore, and of course those who still are.

I'll take you through my football career and all the characters I met, such as Terry Venables, Malcolm Allison, George Best, Sir Bobby Robson, Harry Redknapp, and a cast of thousands, plus the adventures I had along the way.

I'm also going to share my passion for the world of entertainment and showbiz that includes a 'what might have been' music career, a business partnership with David Gest, and stories about Billy Connolly, Mick Jagger, Michael Jackson, Billy Ocean, Shalamar, as well as managing the likes of Alexander O'Neal and Mike Tyson, and my close friendship with Billy Ocean, Dionne Warwick and, well, the list goes on and on.

You'll also discover the inside world of what it's really like being a football agent – one of the UK's most successful, I'm told – and how some of the deals I was involved with panned out, to some of the deals that should have happened but, for reasons that still leave me scratching my head, didn't – and you won't believe some of them!

One thing my life has never been is dull – and I hope by the time you reach the final page, you'll agree.

Time for the curtain to go up. On with the show…

Silks, Somewhere in the Home Counties,
*** June 2024***

Chapter 1

SILK AND STEEL

I come from a warm, loving family background where materialistically we didn't have very much, but in every other aspect we had everything.

It may sound like a bit of a cliché, but in terms of love and support, I was the richest kid in East London. Okay, that does sound like a cliché, but it was a fact.

My mum was called Jane, but known by one and all as Jinny, and her family origins trace back to the Netherlands, where the bloodline of the Kloos family goes back many years. My mum will crop up quite a lot in the early chapters and you'll discover she was an incredible character who had her own – often violent! – way of doing things.

As for my dad – Sam Silkman – his roots are from

Algeria, which is where I get my olive skin and black hair from. My mum had the curls and my dad had very thick, black wavy locks – a good combo for me, so I've been told!

When I first started playing football of any note, people would tell me I'd had a 'Kevin Keegan', meaning I'd based my hairstyle on Keegan's mid-1970s perm that became *de rigueur* in football in the UK at the time, but it wasn't. I'd tell them it was all natural and this was how it had always been – I even suggested maybe he'd based his hairstyle on mine, for all I knew? Whether they believed me or not is another thing…

As a kid, I generally had it cut short, but when I grew it out, back came the curls.

My dad was a painter and decorator – he was a superb wallpaper hanger, which is an art in itself – and my mum was a singer and pianist.

When I was aged around four or five, she'd take me around the pubs and clubs with her. She'd be on the piano, singing away and it wasn't long before she got me up to sing a song or two while she tinkled the ivories. It was there I had my first introduction to show business – and I loved it immediately, finding the applause and attention to be intoxicating.

By day, Mum worked the markets as a stall holder in Petticoat Lane, Spitalfields, which was just a short walk away from our flat in the East End of London. I was an only child. The plan had been that I'd be one of a large brood of Silkman kids but the Second World War came along and by the time it finished, it all seemed too late to start a big family as parents tended to have children young in those days.

In fact, Mum and Dad had resigned themselves to being childless as she was in her late thirties and he was in his mid-forties, but one evening – Dad told me in later years – he went out for a drink with friends, got drunk on Teacher's whisky, returned home a bit amorous and, nine months later, out I popped!

I can't find a logical reason behind it, but as a result – for whatever reason – I can't stand whisky and don't like alcohol full-stop. There must be a connection, but what it is, I haven't a clue. But having said that, I might not be here but for whisky!

So, I entered the world on 29 June, 1952. We lived in a council-owned three-storey-high block made up of two-bedroomed flats – Carter House on Toynbee Street – next door to two of my mum's sisters and their husbands. Completing the family unit was my nan – Julia Kloos – who we initially lived with for a while in my very early years. We were a tight-knit group who may have all lived separately, but we were under one roof and would be in and out of each other's flats all the time.

Mum and Dad never had any money, but I still had the most fantastic childhood. They never once raised a hand to me, never shouted at me and never argued, which is where I get my laidback temperament from. I don't recall one bad memory of them as a child or ever, and even to this day, when I first step out of my house in the morning, I look up at the sky and thank them both for the way they raised me and the beliefs they instilled in me from the second I was born. And also for that unconditional love that is impossible to replace.

They raised me to be generous, loving and very caring, as well as being able to stand up for myself and stand up for the people I love; traits that I, in turn, have passed down to my own kids.

Of course, one particular part of my family has always been the topic of conversation throughout my life: the name Silkman. It's an unusual surname, granted, and the question I am asked most is: are there several generations of Silkmans over in Algeria?

The answer is simple: no.

Silkman is a made-up name; a name that came into being by default via a language misunderstanding, but I'm glad it did because I've always loved being a Silkman. And there is a good and honest reason behind how my surname came to be.

My dad's father arrived in England from Algeria with his wife to seek a new life, but on landing in the UK, the immigration system was nothing like it is today and checks on credentials were, shall we say, a little more lax. His surname was Harar, and he worked as a specialist in silk. As my grandfather's English was poor, when he was filling in the necessary forms on entry to these shores, he thought the line where he put his name was the section he proclaimed his profession. So, under surname he put 'Silk Man' and put 'Harar' under job specification. Because of translation and language issues, he became officially known as Mr Silkman and that was our adopted family name from that moment on. It really was one last Harar for my grandfather!

As a result, everybody with the name Silkman in this country is related in some way or another, because that surname simply didn't exist before.

A little background information never hurts for any story, but now back to the opening words of this book and my first memory of any substance, which I'd love to say was having an ice cream, getting a pet rabbit, or seeing a snowflake fall for the first time – but it actually is pissing myself!

I was two-and-a-half at the time (you'll be glad to hear I wasn't in secondary school when it happened!) and I recall vividly walking from the estate playground towards the entrance to our flats. I was holding an ice lolly in my hand and my mum leaned over the balcony and said, "You alright, boy?"

I looked up and told her about the bad news with my

nether regions warm and on the damp side. I wish it was a different first memory, but there you go!

I wasn't academic in any way or interested in school. I was bright, switched on, but all I wanted to do was sing, run, and play football. I might have looked a bit different from other kids with my Algerian/Dutch DNA, but I never had any issues. It was a multicultural neighbourhood, and we were too focused on just getting by to notice or be bothered by the colour of somebody's skin.

There was an Indian kid called Shaman Wani at my primary school who was one of my best friends, and there were a lot of Jewish kids as well because the East End and Petticoat Lane in particular was predominantly Jewish at that time. The only real difference was I was better looking than most of my peers!

One of my first stage appearances was aged around five when I was sitting with my dad in a club while my mum played on stage. She was a self-taught pianist with a great voice, but partway through her set, she announced to those gathered that her boy was going to come up and sing – I hadn't had a clue she was going to say that, but I was happy to do it. Dressed in shorts and a V-neck cotton patterned top with a gleaming Star of David chain around my neck, I got up to generous applause and went to my mum, where she whispered, "Let's sing 'Rock Around the Clock'."

At that point, I already knew the lyrics to about 150

songs, and Bill Haley and The Comets' worldwide smash was one of my favourites. She played, I sang and a love of performing was born in an instant.

As I sang, the punters started putting money on the stage and by the time I'd finished, Mum told me I'd earned more money for that one song than she'd made all night! My dad gave me a big kiss when I came off to loud cheers and clapping. And I most definitely had been bitten by the showbiz bug – one that has stayed with me throughout my life.

Living in that largely Jewish area, I wasn't aware of any anti-Semitic feeling in my early years. It existed for sure, but it didn't really filter into our daily lives. And where we lived might have been relatively poor, but there was little if any crime in our community and it was a safe place for kids to play out on the streets or walk to the shops and back without parents having to worry.

I would play football on our estate playground until 9.30pm at night and then Mum or Dad would lean over the balcony of the flat and shout me in. Other kids who lived a little further away would know a particular whistle meant it was time to go home and that was how it was. I can't recall any fighting, any gangs or weirdos offering kids sweets, or anyone getting into trouble with the police – nothing at all – it just didn't exist in the area I grew up in back then. It was tight-knit, everyone looked out for each other.

THE NOT SO SECRET FOOTBALL AGENT

My primary school was called Cannon Barnett on Gunthorpe Street, about a five-minute walk from our flat. I hung out mainly with three kids called Michael Martin, Geoffrey Bookman, and Shaman. I was a good sort, a bit mischievous, but polite and always said my pleases and thank yous.

It was so rare that I got told off that I can recall most of the times I got into trouble with vivid clarity.

On one occasion, I remember England were playing a live game in the afternoon, which was a very unusual thing at that time. Geoffrey and I were the best footballers in our school, and we decided we were going to bunk off and not return after the lunch break in order to watch the game, so we went back to my flat and I told my mum and dad we wanted to watch the match. My mum was a huge football fan, and she said it was okay, whereas my dad wasn't that interested in football, but he didn't mind all the same.

The following day, we had to concoct a reason as to why we hadn't attended school in the afternoon. The excuse I gave sounded so viable back then, but now, I can see why the teacher, assistant head Mr Clarke, was trying to suppress a smile. I told him that the belt on my trousers had snapped, and Geoffrey had to hold up one side of my pants all the way home, and as I didn't have another belt we couldn't come back. It was original if nothing else! He grinned and said, "Go on you two, off you go."

My love of football was undoubtedly nurtured by my mum, who was a massive Spurs fan and took me with her to games from the age of about four. We went to see reserve games initially to see how I behaved, then first-team matches at White Hart Lane, and I loved it.

My dad was by then in the rag trade — ladies wear — and had become business partners with a guy called Morris Keston, who was a huge and well-known Spurs fan. Because of Morris, we had people like Ron Henry — a member of the famous 1960-61 Spurs double-winning squad — come to our flat.

Ron had a sidcline in the summer — as players were only paid during the season — and as he was a breeder, we bought a budgerigar from Ron! I met Jimmy Greaves, Danny Blanchflower and other Spurs players too, and it was incredible that I was meeting all these footballers that my mum and I were watching every other Saturday afternoon. I remember Danny putting his arm around me once and saying, "So, what do you want to do when you get older, Barry?"

I said I wanted to either be a singer or a footballer. "Stick to singing," he said. Thankfully, that was because of the wages players got paid back then and not because he'd seen me playing! It was a genuine thrill because I'd been part of the White Hart Lane crowd that had been celebrating winning the double and there must have been 50,000 people chanting, "We want Danny!

We want Danny!" Yet, I wasn't a Spurs fan as such. I suppose they were my team at the time, but when I became a player that association ended, and I would support the team I was playing for.

Though we were a dedicated family of Eastenders, when I was eight we moved to Surrey for a year while my dad opened a ladies wear shop called Sylvia Barry, and it was there that I suppose I first caught the attention of one or two people. At my new school, the football team were training in the playground with a white painted outline of a goal on a shed and mats on the ground for the keeper to dive on.

They were having a shooting practice session and as I was running around with my pals (as I usually was), the ball found its way into my path, so I glanced goalwards and played the ball into the keeper's arms. The teacher who was coaching them shouted, "Stop! Stop! Who are you? What's your name?" I told him I was Barry Silkman and he asked which class I was in. He said, "So you're eight years old? Have you always been able to kick a ball that hard?"

I said, "That wasn't hard. I passed it to him."

He asked if I could hit it harder than I had and I told him that I could. He put the ball on the ground and said, "Okay, hit it towards goal as hard as you can."

I smashed it with power and the keeper turned his back to get out of the way and it smashed into the shed and flew out again. The coach said, "My god. I need to see your teacher. Can you play as good as that?"

I told him I didn't know, and he asked who I was playing for, so I said nobody and that I just played football with my friends.

He said, "Okay, well I'd like you to play for the school team this Saturday. Can you do that?"

So I became the youngest player to play for the Red Lion Yard school team, aged eight – most of the other kids were 10 and 11 – and that is the first time anybody had ever really commented about my football ability. I didn't think much of it.

I knew I could play a bit and now I had a team to play in – and though I started getting attention in games and people saying how good they thought I was, it didn't really register that much. Nothing does when you're eight, does it?

I dreamed of only two things at that point: being a singer or maybe one day even being a footballer – but I didn't know how to progress with either hobby. I was still singing regularly on stage with my mum and loving every minute of it. Everyone told me I had a good voice and I guess if I had a choice at that particular time, singing would have been the pathway I wanted to follow.

But our time in Surrey was short-lived, things didn't work out for my dad as he'd hoped, we returned to the

East End, and I had to leave the school team behind. But I was soon preparing for secondary school in more familiar surroundings after our brief sojourn in the leafy home counties.

Chapter 2

MUM'S THE WORD

Though I hadn't really focused on school and academia, I must have absorbed more than I thought as I sat and passed my 11-plus exam to get into a prestigious school.

I started at Cowper Street Grammar School in September 1963, but I didn't enjoy life there. The day was too structured and obviously, being a grammar school, they pushed you that much harder and they didn't want any slackers.

I just wanted to be with my mates and play football, so I started skipping the odd lesson here and there to play football. I got away with it a couple of times, but my luck finally ran out and I was caught on one occasion and sent to see the headmaster. He was a typically masochistic disciplinarian who read me the riot act before saying, "I'll show you what missing lessons for football results in," before proceeding to give me six of the best against my legs and arse with his cane. I'd never been hit in any form by an adult before and he had struck me with such force, I was in excruciating pain and had massive welts as a result. How did we ever let stuff like that happen in the first place? I'd been wearing school shorts, so when I got home, my mum took one look and asked what I'd done. I told her exactly what had happened, and she said, "What? Right, we're going back to school right now!"

I could see the rage building up inside her. I was thinking, 'Shit. God help him!'

School had finished and everyone had gone home by that stage, so there was nothing she could do immediately. Maybe she'd cool down overnight? Ha, no chance! More likely she stewed overnight and the next morning, however, was a different story. She took me to school, marched me into the head's office and, pointing to my legs, said to him, "What the fuck do you think this is, you no-good cunt? Who the fuck are you to lift a finger towards my son? Well? I know why you've done this. He's the only Jew in this school and that's why you've done this."

She then picked up the cane and hit him across the face with it. He reeled to one side, and she did it again, knocking him to the floor where she proceeded to beat the shit out of the headmaster with his own cane all over his body until he was screaming for her to stop. Eventually, he got up and as he stood, she punched him in the mouth and he staggered back, with blood coming out of his mouth and nose.

"My boy's never coming to this fucking school again and if I ever see you again outside, I'll fucking do the same again. Come on, boy." And we left.

She was a hard bastard who could more than take care of herself and she wouldn't take shit off anybody.

My dad was the calmest, quietest man on the planet, but cross my mum and you'd know about it. And if anyone touched her boy, you'd better start running and be quick, too.

She carried a flick-knife with her wherever she went, and I remember another time when she'd been out to bingo in Hackney and I was on my way home. As I approached our flats, I saw a man running in my direction, screaming, and holding the side of his face. Blood was pumping out. He ran past and I then heard my mum yelling, "Come back here you bastard!"

What had happened was she had got off the bus and this guy got off as well. She was certain he was following her and that something was going to happen, and when she reached the lift at our flats — we lived on the 14th floor — she felt a tap on her shoulder. She turned around and it was the same man, with his cock out and mac open to show her. She was ready for him, had taken her blade out already and slashed his cheek wide open.

As he ran for his life, she screamed out, "Come back here you cunt! I'm not finished with you!"

Probably not what he'd been expecting, it's fair to say, but boy did he pick the wrong woman that night. As you might imagine, we never saw him again, but somewhere in East London, there was a man with a six-inch scar down his cheek as a permanent reminder of the night he met Jinny Kloos.

She later told me she would have cut his cock off had she caught up with him, and I've no doubt she would have.

She never took any shit from anyone and for me, that was a powerful role model to have. I suppose it's not that common to have a mum that hardened gangsters would think twice about dealing with, but to me it was normal, and she would act first and ask questions later if she felt she or anyone close to her had been wronged.

I recall she was once working on a stall for a guy called Maurice Simons in Petticoat Lane. I was about 14 and on the stall with her when a man and a woman came by, perusing the clothes she was selling. She had a sign up saying 'One dress for £3.50 or two for £6'.

The woman eventually found a dress she liked and held it up to her husband and told my mum she'd take it. Mum asked if she wanted the hanger as well, and the woman said she did. Mum wrapped it up and asked for the £3.50 but the guy said he only wanted to pay £3. Mum said he'd need to get two items for them to be £3 each because of the discount she was offering, but he was insistent that he wasn't paying more than £3 for the one dress. She'd handed the dress to him before he started haggling, so she took it back out of his hands, to which he responded, "All you Jews should have been gassed in Germany." Not the wisest words he had ever spoken, I'm certain.

Mum dropped the dress, swung around, and punched him under the chin, and he went down, banged his head on the pavement and was out cold. His wife, stupidly, went for my mum and she ended up having her nose split wide open as my mum butted her square in the face. The bloke was snoring on the deck, the woman had blood pouring out of her nose and mum shouted, "Now tell me the Jews should have all been fucking gassed in Germany you dirty bastards!"

The police soon turned up, took the couple and my mum away, but an hour later she was back on the stall and had been released without charge, which was something of a miracle. I still don't know how she got away with that, but she did – it could have been that the couple were too frightened to press charges, but she never said.

Mum also took part in a march against the Blackshirt Movement in the 1930s, where Jewish people and black people protested against British supporters of the Nazis. Known, I think, as The Battle of Cable Street, around 3,000 Blackshirt members were confronted by more than 150,000 anti-fascists – my mum included – and there were violent clashes throughout the East End, which was predominantly Jewish.

It was horrific by all accounts and my mum – who carried a 10-inch blade with her – says she slashed one Blackshirt supporter after another in the chaos, but woke up in hospital with a knife wound from her shoulder down to her hand after she'd been attacked.

Historians claim there was little violence, but my mum said it was out of control and it was horrific.

She was a lunatic, but she didn't care about anyone other than her family. Her maiden name, as stated earlier, was Kloos and you'd hear people say, "Don't mess with Jinny Kloos – she'll kill you."

I loved her to pieces and though we never had a pot to piss in, I never went without food or clothes.

Mum and Dad would do anything for anyone, they were kind and generous, but they could look after themselves and God help anyone who threatened or tried to harm me. I believe they would have killed to protect me, particularly my mum who was a wonderful woman.

But the fact is, Jews still faced terrible abuse and, in my eyes, still do. How many Jewish footballers are there in this country? How many Jewish managers are there? How many Jews are part of the FA? We are the forgotten minority, but you don't hear people protesting or shouting from the rooftops that there should be more Jews involved in football. It pisses me off no end and has done throughout my life and I'm still waiting for somebody to shout our corner and fight for our cause. And do you know why? The last top-flight English-born Jewish professional footballer we had in this country was me! We can't all be fucking useless, surely?

I digress. Back to school…

I was glad to be away from the grammar school and instead started at Robert Montefiore School, Vallance Road, in Whitechapel where I'd remain until I left school at the age of 15.

I loved every minute of it.

We moved home quite a bit for a few years, but always remained in the East End where our family and friends were.

I continued playing football for my school team, playing anywhere and everywhere, but I didn't like tackling so I was never going to be a defender. I loved watching all sorts of players such as Cliff Jones, John

White, Danny Blanchflower, Jimmy Greaves, and others. I didn't base my style on anyone but the way I did play was probably a reflection of my personality. I had no aim or goal in mind, and I wasn't working to a plan. I guess I was just drifting happily along, content with life and not thinking too far ahead. No scouts came to watch me. I was doing okay, but it was all just for fun.

Then, one time, my dad went to a boxing match and met a guy called Dave Glazer who was a scout for QPR. My dad told him, "My boy is a really good footballer, you know?"

Dave said, "Really? Every father thinks their son is a good footballer."

Dad said, "Yeah, but I don't know anything about football. I'm just saying what everybody else tells me."

Dave smiled and promised Dad he'd take a look at me. He invited me to a school in Putney where there were a couple of pitches, and I was to play in an eight-a-side match. I must have scored about 10 goals, but the quality of the lads I was playing with was hopeless. I was thinking that if this was what professional football was all about, I'd probably be in the QPR first team the weekend after! Dave didn't say much as he gave me a lift home, but he came up to the flat with me and spoke to my parents.

He said, "I'll tell you what's happened. I put him with the lads who are never gonna be any good, but we keep them on so they have something to do. I didn't want to pitch him in with the better players in case he struggled, but he's miles better than them, so next week he'll be training with the proper players around his age group."

And that was the start of it. Nothing spectacular, no big fanfare or anything – I just sort of ambled into football.

I went along and trained with QPR as a 16-year-old and though it didn't feel like it at the time, the start of my 55-year association with professional football had begun.

Chapter 3

THE (NOT SO) ARTFUL DODGIN

I settled in well at QPR and was soon playing regular reserve-team football for them during the 1968-69 season, but then the coach Alec Stock was sacked and Bill Dodgin Junior took over. It didn't take him long to make it perfectly clear that he had a big problem with me. So much so that the other lads commented on it with one saying, "Jesus, Silks – why does Bill fucking hate you?"

I couldn't figure it out, but he was always picking on me for one reason or another. I remember scoring in one game and afterwards, Dodgin said, "You're only in it for you."

THE (NOT SO) ARTFUL DODGIN

I said, "How do you mean? I scored a goal."

He said, "Yes, but it was the wrong thing to do. You should have passed it across the goal for your team-mate."

On my way home, I was trying to figure out how scoring a goal could be the wrong thing to do? It was clear that whatever I did, it was going to be wrong in his eyes, so I decided it was better for me to move on. In fact, that was the only reason I decided to leave QPR – Bill Dodgin. When your manager doesn't like you for reasons I assumed were other than footballing ones, there's nowhere really to go and it won't be you that wins.

Word in football travels fast, especially between clubs that are two miles apart, and a chief scout at Fulham – Kenny Craggs – had once told me he loved me as a player and when he learned I was leaving QPR, he invited me to Fulham who were keen to sign me on as an apprentice. But I wasn't interested in cleaning boots and sweeping dressing room floors. It just wasn't for me.

All I wanted to do was improve my skills and become a better footballer. I didn't see how doing any of the other stuff benefited me, so I declined the offer of an apprenticeship. Manager Bobby Robson told me he respected my decision and if that was the case, they would instead sign me on as a professional on my 18th birthday, which was 29 June, 1970. The plan was to put pen to paper on 1 July – but that was still a while away.

I immediately liked Bobby Robson and he took me out to Dusseldorf in Germany, where we won a tournament, and I did well whenever I was used. By the time we returned, Robson told me he was going to start playing me in the reserves and Billy Gray, his assistant, came around to see Mum and Dad, have a chat about what the club's plans were and keep them in the picture. He told them he thought I was the most talented lad they had at the club. "You just need to give him a kick up the arse to work harder and we can get him into the first team," he told them.

Former England World Cup winner George Cohen was our youth team coach with George Milton alongside him for my first season, so I was surrounded by some fantastic personalities with a wealth of knowledge and experience, and I felt really at home at Craven Cottage.

I remember one incident I had at the club that you'd get crucified for in today's controlled, cameras-everywhere environment. That's the thing, back then, you could get away with murder – not literally, of course – but some of the chances you took were ridiculous, but they seemed fine at the time.

I'd picked up an injury but was recovering well and nearing full fitness. I called up the physio and said I was alright to start playing again and he just said, "No, no – you've got to rest some more."

I'd been chatting with a mate of mine who played for

THE (NOT SO) ARTFUL DODGIN

Grays Athletic, and he said, "Why don't you come and play for us this weekend? The manager would love to have you and we can play you under another name."

I thought, 'why not?' – I could improve my fitness and as this was several decades before mobile phones and social media, the chances of me getting found out were slim. The Grays boss was called Tommy Harris, and his claim to fame was that his son was one of the first Milky Bar Kids – Steve 'Milky' Harris.

I went along to training on the Thursday night where it had started to get really foggy, and afterwards I went into the club house bar for an orange juice. While I was there, in walks the Milky Bar Kid. I was thinking of something witty to say, but decided the poor lad must have heard just about everything and left it. Tommy Harris asked me if I would play at the weekend, and that they could use another player's name on the team sheet, so I said I would. Why not? It would help my match sharpness and be a bit of fun. I'd maybe even be set for Milky Bars for life!

One of the lads offered to give me a lift to Grays railway station, but the fog had got worse, so he started driving slowly out of the club car park looking for the main road. Visibility was down to a couple of yards and the ground under the car felt odd. I asked him to stop so I could get out and try to get my bearings and as I did, I noticed there was grass under my feet, and I looked to my right and was face to face with a cow! We were in the middle of a herd of cows, and it took us about 30 minutes to find our way out of the field.

I played for Grays at the weekend and enjoyed it, scoring one goal and making another, but I overheard a woman near the tunnel as I passed say, "He looks just like the guy who was playing for Fulham Reserves a few weeks back." Everyone was saying I should come and play for Grays permanently and I was like, "But I'm at Fulham! I love it here but why would I swap Fulham for non-league?"

And that was the end of my cameo at Grays but, as I say, I don't think I'd get away with doing that today.

So, misdemeanours aside, life at the Cottage was great.

There was one occasion when the first team had an evening game and I finished training in the morning, and because I had no other means of transport I took the train home from Fulham Broadway afterwards.

When I got home, my mum told me I'd had a phone call to say I was in the first team squad for the game later on. I asked how many they said were named and she said 13, which basically meant they just wanted me to put the boots out. But there was a chance I might be on the bench, so I told her I'd better get prepared because there was a chance I might get an extra £2 appearance bonus. A couple of hours later, I was ready

THE (NOT SO) ARTFUL DODGIN

to travel back to Craven Cottage and as I was about to leave, my mum said, "Where are you going? You can't go dressed like that."

I asked her what she was talking about as I was wearing a jacket, shirt, tie, and trousers. She said I needed to put a really nice suit on so I said again, "Mum, what are you talking about?"

She said, "Well, you don't look smart enough and if you don't, you won't get your appearance fee."

The penny dropped. I said, "Do you know what appearance money means? It means if you play for the first team – appear for the team in other words."

She said, "Ah, I thought it was money they gave you for how you looked."

Priceless.

But two thirds through my first year, Robson was sacked, and Johnny Haynes took temporary control until a new manager was brought in during the summer. At least that was the plan, but he only lasted a month before he'd had enough. I spoke with Kenny Craggs about my situation as obviously it had been Robson that had agreed I would sign professional forms in the summer, and he said not to worry, we'd have a new manager coming in soon and I'd be turning pro as planned the following July.

What was about to happen, however, was the worst case scenario – for me at least.

It was the start of December 1968. We were all told to get to the ground and wait in the dressing room for an announcement. There were dozens of journalists everywhere and we got wind that a new manager had been appointed but hadn't a clue who it was. Next thing, the dressing door opens and who walks in? Bill Dodgin. I couldn't believe it. Kenny Craggs took him around to shake each of the players' hands and as he got to me, Kenny said, "This is Barry Silkman and he'll be signing pro forms on 1 July."

He just looked at me and said, "Yeah, I know all about him. I'll speak to you later."

He completely fucking ignored me. It was a nightmare. The other lads asked me what that had all been about and when Dodgin left the dressing room, Kenny came back and said, "Fuck me, Silks – what the fuck's going on? He's saying he doesn't think you're ready to sign professional yet we think you're ready for the first team."

I explained to Kenny what had happened at QPR, and I knew now that my days at Fulham were numbered. I hadn't been able to figure out exactly why Dodgin hated me so much – until one day when we were having a game of cricket at the Cottage. There was a big wall where the turnstiles are today, and a set of wickets painted on it where we used to have the odd game. George Cohen was batting. Dodgin must gave seen us playing but because I was under the cottage stairs fielding, he must

THE (NOT SO) ARTFUL DODGIN

have thought I'd gone. He shouted down to George, "Whoever heard of a Yid boy playing cricket?"

I came out from under the stairs and the game stopped – but what happened next is something I would rather not go into, but let's just say he wasn't in the best physical condition by the time I'd finished. Save to say I was kicked out of football for a year. Had it happened today, that sort of anti-Semitic statement would have seen Dodgin kicked out of football for good. But that is now, this was then – and I was out.

No club would touch me, because of what had happened, and I was *persona non grata* for a year, so I decided that was the end of my football career and that I was best focusing on a life away from the game. I went back to singing in nightclubs, which I'd been doing off and on for a few years by that point. I was getting paid for it by night and by day I tried a variety of jobs, including working at a stockbrokers, a role at an analysis company and, if all else failed, I'd work on the stalls at Petticoat Lane as I had done as a kid with my mum. Being a footballer seemed like the last thing I'd be doing for a living as I tried to figure out what came next…

Chapter 4

TV TIMES

I'd been playing two or three games a week to keep myself fit and because I just loved playing the game, just like any other 19-year-old with football in their blood. I was enjoying myself, playing with my mates and in one Sunday League match I scored four goals and made four more in a 9-2 win – I think the team was called Stepney Lads. I think there were one or two comments of 'ringer', but I wasn't with a club, so why not?

It was pretty standard fayre to be honest as the truth was – with no arrogance – I was a very good footballer playing at a very low level.

As I trudged off the pitch, there was a guy standing ahead of me, obviously looking to engage in conversation. I expected a 'decent game, mate' or similar but he just said in a broad Scottish accent, "What are you doing playing Sunday League, son? You're much, much better than this."

I knew I was, but it was decent of him to say.

I just said thanks for the kind words, but he said, "Look, my name is Eddie McCullum and I've discovered a lot of players in my time, and I think you should be playing professional football. I've got a close friend who has just taken over at Wimbledon called Mike Everett, and there are other players I've found for him who are playing there now and I'd like to invite you to training one day next week if you are interested?"

I said I'd love to, went along for one session, and at the end the manager told me he'd like to sign me on until the end of the season and he added that he'd like to put me straight in the team for the next game. It had all happened pretty quickly, but I was back in football, albeit at Southern League level.

They were paying me £5 a week plus a couple more quid for travel, which was fine by me – a bit of pocket money if nothing else!

Wimbledon had a winger called David Armstrong who was rapid, and he told me he'd help make me a great player. "Just knock it into space down the flank and I'll catch it – what happens after that, I haven't a clue, but I'll definitely catch it," he said.

He was as good as his word, and we struck up a

great understanding. Word was getting around about this curly-haired, olive-skinned teenager strutting his stuff for Wimbledon and a number of scouts started watching me. I was out of contract at the end of the season, so there would be no fee to pay and a few of those monitoring me must have been thinking I might be worth a gamble.

Mike Everett pulled me to one side at the end of the season and told me he'd love me to stay, but also revealed that Barnet wanted to sign me. They were a bigger club – in the same division but in a better spot financially – and were offering double the money I was on with Wimbledon, plus travel expenses. My belief in the game was coming back. I never doubted my own ability and started to think maybe I could make a living out of football after all. I'd just sort of lost my way and the momentum I'd had with what had happened at Fulham.

Of course, being a flair player in a tough working class league, I got kicked to pieces week in, week out, but I could hold my own. I'd get elbowed in the face, kneed in the back and was on the end of what you might call numerous industrial challenges. But I was an East End lad and my mum had taught me a trick or two!

The Wimbledon fans had taken to me because I loved to play football and that meant flicks, tricks, scooping it over defenders' heads, juggling the ball on the touchline – they loved all that and I loved doing it. If I could entertain, I wasn't interested! Fortunately, the manager encouraged me to express myself and I had team-mates telling me to try particular moves in games such as flicking over an opponent's head and catching it between my knees on the other side. I'm sure they had a private sweepstake going to see what I could do!

Gerry Ward was the Barnet manager and in my first conversation with him, he said, "I'd absolutely love it if you came and played for me, and I believe I can get you back into league football."

That was enough for me – plus the additional wages – and I signed a two-year contract with Barnet.

Gerry left the club shortly after I'd signed and Gordon Ferry took over, but things still went really well for me. Barnet had two former players called Ricky George and Billy Meadows who were determined to get me back playing league football again, so I had the adulation of the fans, the support of the manager and my team-mates and people in and around the club, and I felt they were all pulling in my direction because they felt I deserved better than playing Southern League football.

Looking back, there was an incident at Barnet that still makes me smile today. In fact, it's so off the charts from today's game and the ultra-professional world we call elite sports that it might seem hard to believe – but each and every word of the following is true, believe me.

I was friendly with a girl called Diane Smyth and her father was a well-known horse trainer called Ron Smyth. They told me about a horse they really fancied that was running in the November Manchester Handicap.

It would race on the upcoming Saturday at 3.30 – by which time Barnet would be playing a match away to Grantham Town (I think). The Smyths had already given us a tip on a horse they had the week before – Flash Imp – and they felt that had a chance, so some of the lads had backed it as part of a double. It had come in at 28/1, so the money the lads won would go on this other tip I'd been given called Only For Joe, ridden by a jockey called Ian Jenkinson.

I desperately wanted to see the race, so I said I had picked up a knock because I wanted to watch the race and Ian Fusedale was too nervous to play and was named as the 14th man for the game because he had a huge amount of money riding on Only For Joe. The players all wanted to know the result of the race as soon as it ended, so Ian listened on a transistor radio and after about five minutes, he jumps up on the sidelines shouting, "It's won, it's won!" Bear in mind there were about 2,000 people watching the game, totally mystified as our players started leaping up, punching the air, hugging each other.

The ball had been in our possession, but the lads just left it! The referee stopped the game because he thought something had happened and was totally confused by it all.

The manager at the time, Gordon Ferry, never touched the horses but he'd put a wager on it and came running on the pitch. It must have looked hysterical. It had come in at 14/1 and the lads won a small fortune on it, including Ian Fusedale who built an extension to his house with the winnings. Ricky George and Ian bought me an 18-carat gold watch as a present for sharing the tip. Great days.

In 1974, Ricky told me they had spoken with Colin Addison, manager of Hereford United, and convinced him he had to sign me at the end of my first season with Barnet. They told me Hereford would pay a fee for me – I never found out how much – and I jumped at the chance to get back into league football.

But yet again, as had happened so often before, the manager I'd agreed to sign for was gone by the time I arrived! It was bizarre how many times it had happened, and Addison had been replaced by John Sillett. I met John and his first words were, "I don't know you, I've not had any part of this, and I can't sign you."

I was thinking, I'm sure I've heard this before!

He added, "What I can do is have you over on a trial

and spend the first two weeks of pre-season with us and if I like the look of you, I'll sign you."

I didn't know what to do – go back to Barnet or stay where I was and give it a go. I had made the journey, so I thought I might as well try. I got along really well with some of the Hereford lads – Dixie McNeil, Steve Emery and Tommy Hughes – and training went really well for the first week. We had a friendly match and afterwards Sillett came up to me and told me he was happy to sign me on as a Hereford United player. But he had a caveat…

"I want you to stop taking the piss," he said. "Half the time you're on the pitch is spent taking the piss out of the opposition."

I said, "That's because they're not very good."

He just started laughing and shook his head. Looking back, I still can't for the life of me understand why he did sign me because if you wanted to find a footballer who was everything John Sillett didn't want in a player, it was Barry Silkman.

I got on amazingly well with him outside of football with our shared love of horse racing, but inside football I had no relationship with him at all.

I stayed in digs which were weird to say the least. Half of the tenants were normal everyday people you'd find in a guesthouse and the rest were what we used to call dossers! It was okay but a bit strange, and after a while Dixie and his wife Dana took me in as a lodger in their spare room, which was fantastic because he was a smashing lad and a terrific goalscorer.

Hereford is sort of in the sticks, especially if you're a lad from the East End of London, but I was determined to try and make it as a footballer, so I was happy to go with the flow. I didn't mind a bit and the local ladies seemed to like this chirpy, curly-haired Cockney lad! I was on £40 a week and my parents were subsidising me. Not that they had much money themselves, but they knew this was my dream and did whatever they could to help make it happen. I had to put my singing career on hold, but it was good to be kicking a ball around again.

Dixie and I would go to the greyhound racing in Gloucester once a week and usually end up in a nightclub called Tracey's afterwards. I'd always leave with a pretty girl on my arm, and I always acted like an absolute gentleman around them.

I was doing well enough at Hereford, but I knew I frustrated the hell out of Sillett because of how I played the game. One thing I've always prided myself on is being a fantastic judge of a footballer. That would come into use later in my life, but I could just spot someone who was destined for bigger and better things. A case in point was when we came up against Mansfield Town in back-to-back games in February 1976.

Mansfield, as I recall, were bottom of the table and

as we were joint-top, we were expected to win both games comfortably. But they were battering us in every sense other than the scoreline and we were being totally outplayed.

I said to Dixie as we came off at the break, "How the fuck are this lot bottom? They just killed us."

We were drawing 1-1 at our place and went back to the dressing room where John Sillett came in raging with the veins on his neck pulsating and his eyes bulging because they had murdered us. We ended up drawing the game 2-2 and went back into the changing rooms where Sillett went mental again. He couldn't believe we'd been held by a team at the foot of the table who had been the better team for much of the game. He went berserk and then he looked straight at me and said, "And you? I suppose you think they're a fucking good team?"

I had Dixie on one side of me and on the other was player-coach Terry Payne – both top players coming towards the end of their careers and both experienced enough to know what was coming. Terry kicked my leg as if to say, 'For fuck's sake, don't say anything!' and Dixie pinched a hair on my leg more or less trying to hint the same thing.

But it made no difference, because when I had something to say, more often than not, I said it. "Well, to be honest gaffer, I think they are the best team we've played this season. And their striker is the best forward we've come up against."

I watched all the boys' heads drop and stare at the floor.

Sillett was apoplectic.

"You fucking cunt!" he shouted. "What do you know about football, you fucking idiot!"

He then picked up the big tin pot of tea and launched it towards the bathroom where it smashed into a wall and water and teabags flew everywhere. "You know fuck all!"

He stormed out, slamming the door behind him and Dixie looked at me and said, "Silks, why the fuck did you say that?"

I told him I'd said what I said because I genuinely did think they'd been the best team we'd played. As it happened, we beat them 1-0 four days later – but they then went on an unbeaten run of 19 games, winning 12 and drawing seven to finish eleventh in the league, not that far behind the teams that went up.

They were the form team of the division and that striker I liked who played for them? Ray Clarke – he ended up playing for Tottenham.

We won the league that season and got promoted and I remember being called into Sillett's office where he said, "Look Silks, I'm going to be honest – I don't want to keep you, but Terry Venables has just taken over at Crystal Palace and he wants to make you his first signing if you're interested? He wants you so you can go there with my blessing."

I was more than happy with that and as I turned to leave his office, he said, "Silky, you were right about Mansfield. What a team they are and that striker? What a player!" I said nothing and just walked out smiling.

I've always been able to spot a really good player – many people might say the same – but seeing something in a player and what they are capable of is something I've always prided myself on. Ray Clarke was a top striker, but I don't think he'd scored that many goals up to that point, so it wasn't as obvious as it would be by the end of the season.

But I would spot players again and again and maybe that's why I ended up becoming a football agent.

What disappointed me the most about my exit from Hereford was that they took away the only medal I would win in my career, and winning Division Three might not register with some people but it meant a lot to me.

After the last game of the season, we had a charity match at Edgar Street and a chance to celebrate our promotion with our supporters. We were each presented with our winner's medal and wore them around our necks while photographs were taken, and we walked around the pitch on a kind of lap of honour. The medals were then all collected to be taken to an engraver to be inscribed with our names and the achievement of winning the league.

Because that was my last game of any sort for the club, I obviously wasn't around to collect my medal when they were returned from the engravers. I contacted the club to find out where my medal was so they could send it on but was told the manager had given it to one of his backroom staff instead. That pissed me off no end.

I thought that was really poor and I can't understand why they did that.

That was the end of my time at Hereford United and I have to say, in spite of the odd bollocking and that lost medal, I really enjoyed my time there. They gave me a peg up to get back into league football and I'd like to think I did my bit by helping them win promotion. It just shouldn't have ended the way it did.

Meanwhile, Aldershot had also got wind of my availability and called me to say they would love to sign me as well, but Palace's chief scout, Arnie Warren, got in touch to invite me to Selhurst Park to meet Terry and there would never be any competition between Aldershot and Palace.

So I went back to London and met Terry. He said, "Look, I really want to sign you on, so come on pre-season with us to Holland and we can talk finances and discuss everything."

I was happy with that, liked Terry immediately and went to Holland with Palace and, as there were no agents back then, Terry and I chatted about salary and length of contract. He told me he was selling his best player, Peter Taylor, who was signing for Spurs for £400,000 – and added he wanted me to replace Taylor as the star of his team. I said, "TV, now I really know you're a good judge of a player," and he just laughed.

I played the first friendly and did exceptionally well but got a kick in my back in training and missed the next game. I played in the final tour match and did really well again, so TV said he needed to get my contract sorted to get me on board officially.

So, how does a player go from Hereford United to a club the size of Palace – and be tasked with replacing their best player? And how did TV even know who I was?

The answer to the last one is that he'd known me from being 11 years old, when he was a Spurs player. Morris Keston, that well-known and well-connected Spurs superfan and business partner of my dad that I mentioned earlier, was forever telling TV that his friend's son was going to be a fantastic footballer. Terry even came along to watch me playing in the playground as a kid and I suppose he just kept an eye on me and my career.

When he got the job at Palace – his first in management – he asked Arnie Warren to find one or two players who could really build the club up but were maybe under the radar so wouldn't cost too much.

Arnie told him, "There's this one player at Hereford, I think you'll love him. He's called Barry Silkman."

TV said, "Oh my god – Silky? I've known him since he was a kid – and I loved him as a kid."

Arnie said, "I think you'll love him even more now."

And on that basis, I became TV's first ever signing.

I was heading back to London. I was going from playing in front of 4,000 people to a club that regularly attracted 25,000. Palace were a club that were on a completely different level in terms of size and standing. It was really strange in many ways, and I couldn't quite get my head around it. But I wasn't complaining. I was back home again and playing for a manager who didn't mind a bit of flair; he demanded it!

Chapter 5

CRYSTAL CLEAR

I would say my time with Crystal Palace was the most enjoyable of my playing career.

In Terry Venables – 'TV' to me – I had a kindred spirit because he was into so much more than just football and he would open up a whole new world to me with his show business connections and friends. In fact, he told me I was more suited to the show business world because of my personality, and the thing I liked most about him was that he loved to sing as much as I did!

Palace had just been relegated under Malcolm Allison, but they had some terrific players. They had the likes of Jimmy Cannon, Ian Evans, Dave Swindlehurst, and I felt at home straight away. TV and I had a fantastic relationship and I think I reminded him a bit of himself when he was younger. He was a part-time singer and an entrepreneur, and he had a lot of fingers in a lot of pies – plus so many connections in the entertainment industry. He trusted my football judgement, too.

"You could always spot a player, Silks," he said. "I remember some of the players you talked about a few years back, and they all went on to do well, so give me your opinion on someone."

He had tried this player he was talking about at centre-half, centre-midfield and as a striker, and he just couldn't figure out where he would be best utilised, so a week later, as we walked in off the training pitch, I said, "TV – the answer is right-back." He asked me what I meant, and I told him the player he'd asked me to watch, that he should play him as a right-back.

He laughed and said he would never make a right-back, so I asked him to stop, close his eyes and listen to me tell him all the things he was good at, and when I'd finished I asked him which position I had just described. He said, "A right-back." So, we went on pre-season to Holland and in the dressing room before the game, Terry looked at the player – Paul Hinshelwood – and told him he'd be playing right-back that day. He said, "Gaffer, I've never played there before…" Terry looked at me and said, "If it doesn't work, blame him!" and pointed at me.

Hinshelwood went on to play more than 300 games for Palace in that position.

Soon after, he said, "I want you to have a look at this 17-year-old kid we've got. He's a left-back and I'm thinking of making him a first-team regular."

So, I kept a close eye on this lad for a few training sessions and it wasn't long before I told TV not to hesitate – I loved this kid and could see he had what it took. I knew he was going to go to the top. It was Kenny Sansom, who would go on to win 86 caps for England.

Another time, I helped TV sign a keeper. I'd been on holiday in Morocco and gone running every morning to keep sharp. On one of my runs one day, I met a goalkeeper called John Burridge, who was at Aston Villa at the time, and also on holiday. We got talking and he said, "Can't you get Terry to sign me?" 'Budgie' was a lunatic trainer, but he wasn't very tall for a keeper – maybe five foot nine inches, though he had an incredible leap, was athletic and agile.

I didn't think much more about it; he went back to Villa, and I went back to Palace. Budgie couldn't get a game with Villa because Jimmy Rimmer was playing so well, so he went on loan to Southend, just so he could put himself in the shop window. He called me up and asked me to go and see him play, which I did, and I loved what I saw. I went back to Palace and told TV we should sign him, and he said, "Yeah, I've been told about him but also that he's nowhere near good or big enough."

I said, "TV, trust me, you'll love him."

A few days later, TV said that he, myself, and his assistant manager Alan Harris were going to watch Burridge play as Southend were at home on a Friday evening. I drove to Roots Hall, and we sat in the directors' box, but I hadn't told Budgie we were coming. About 20 minutes had been played and Budgie hadn't had a shot to save or pretty much anything to do and TV said, "I can't judge him on this."

Then, Southend conceded a corner and as it came in, there was a header that was going well wide, but Budgie leapt across to his right and gathered the ball – a 'one for the cameras' type of dive. TV looked at me and said, "What's he doing?"

Next thing, Budgie jumped up and threw the ball like an arrow out to the right-winger Tony Towner, who beat the full-back, crossed it in and the Southend centre-forward scored, all in a matter of about 10 seconds. I looked at TV and said, "Now you know why…"

He said, "Silks, I've seen enough. Have you got his number?"

I said I had the hotel number he was staying at. He said, "Good, call him later and tell him we're going to sign him."

Budgie was soon in goal for us, and the fans loved

him – I think we were 4-0 up against Ipswich Town once and he climbed up and sat on his crossbar because he was bored. He'd do his handstands and God knows what else, but he was a great goalie as well as being an entertainer.

We finished just below mid-table in 1976-77, but after that first season, things began to change for me a bit at Palace, partly because of my life outside the football world.

I was still loving my time at the club and in my playing career, and always loved playing at Selhurst Park. I even loved the kit! But I loved singing, too, and after training, four or five times a week I'd head to the recording studio to sing, whether that was backing vocals or whatever. TV was well aware of it and actively encouraged it because of his passion for singing, so it was never a problem for me or him.

We'd done well enough in the league, held our own and I had made a good contribution, but TV said that he was going to change things around a bit for the 1979-80 season and, ultimately, that resulted in me playing less and less. I couldn't get my head around it because I'd done as much as anyone in the team, I had a fantastic relationship with the fans, and TV – but my opportunities became fewer and fewer.

I guess things sort of came to a head when I travelled to Selhurst Park for a midweek game against Aston

Villa and TV took me to one side and said, "How are you feeling, Silks?" I told him I felt brilliant, and he said, "Good – I want you to go out and rip this lot to pieces tonight."

So, not long after, I went into the dressing room where there were 13 of us in there and TV walks in, announces the team – and I'm not in it! I wasn't even on the bench! I was wondering what the fuck that was all about. He didn't even speak to me about it, yet just half an hour before he'd told me he wanted me to tear the opposition apart! It was bizarre, and as much as I loved TV, it sort of made my mind up that it was probably time to move on.

I was sitting in the stands watching the game and Palace were 4-0 down to Villa when Malcolm Allison came over and said hello. He was puffing away on one of his Cuban cigars and he said, "Silky, I'm at Plymouth and I want you to come and sign for us on loan. I'm serious and I want to build the team around you, and everyone will love you down there."

It was out of the blue and sort of took me by surprise. I said, "I'm not sure, Malcolm, I don't know what I'm going to do next."

He said, "Look, come on loan, find out if you like it or not and if you do, we can make it permanent." So I said, "Yeah, why not?"

So, within a few days a loan deal had been struck

and before I headed to Devon, TV stopped me in the corridor at Selhurst and asked why I'd been happy to go out on loan. I said, "TV, you weren't playing me, and I need to play."

He said that he might not have been picking me, but he would have done if I'd spoken to him and told him how I was feeling. It was an odd exchange, especially after that Villa game, but it was also too late because I was happy to go and get some game time with Malcolm and take on a fresh challenge.

I went to Plymouth where my loan spell would cover five games, but after just three appearances I knew it felt right and told Malcolm I was happy to move if they still wanted to buy me. He said the players and fans loved me, and he'd get the deal done.

I moved to a guest house in Plymouth initially before moving to a hotel while I looked for my own place. In the meantime, Malcolm left Argyle for Manchester City. It had happened again! I had only been at Home Park for a couple of months and the man who had believed in me enough to say he would build the team around me had gone, and a guy called Bobby Saxton took over. I didn't know Bobby from Adam, but my arrangement with Malcolm was that I went back to London after each Saturday match, had Sunday and Monday off and returned for training on Tuesday at 1pm.

Everything had changed so fast that after the match

on Saturday, Malcom left and was replaced by Monday morning – there was no Sky Sports, nobody had told me, and the jungle drums were silent.

I was at home in London when my phone went on the Monday afternoon. I answered it and a voice said, "Is that Barry Silkman?" I told him it was. The voice said, "Barry, this is Bobby Saxton." I was a bit nonplussed but just said hello and asked what I could do for him. He said, "Do you know who I am? I'm the new manager of Plymouth Argyle." I asked where Malcolm was, and he told me Malcolm had left the day before. It was the first I'd heard! "Where are you?" he asked. "You didn't show up for training this morning."

I told him of the arrangement I had with Malcolm, and he said, "Yeah, but I'm not Malcolm." I hadn't even been told Malcolm had left. It was fair to say Bobby and I hadn't got off to the best start, and yet again the writing seemed to be on the wall for me before I'd even had the chance to play for him.

I was regularly going back to London to see my girlfriend and I was mixing more and more in showbiz circles and was good friends with Kenny Lynch, Jess Conrad, Bill Kenwright, plus a whole host of actors and singers. I was getting invited to lots of parties and events and I really enjoyed that being part of my life.

I was driving back to Plymouth at 2am sometimes in my Daimler Jaguar, so it was lucky I was so fit and never drank a drop of alcohol – I never have as it doesn't agree with me – and I could get by on six hours of sleep, so nobody knew what I was doing when I was away from the club.

I returned to Home Park on the Tuesday morning for training and Bobby Saxton called me into his office because I'd been told he wanted a word with me. I thought, 'here we go again…' I went in, and Bobby was sat behind his desk, so I reached over to shake his hand, but he didn't reciprocate. I was thinking, 'Okay, fair enough, if that's the path we're going to go down…'

And then he began.

"Look, let's get this straight," he said. "You're Malcolm Allison's player, not mine, and as far as I'm concerned, if Malcolm comes in for you, you can just go. I don't particularly want you here."

Okay…

I thought for a moment and said, "Let me tell you something, Bob – I'm not calling you boss or gaffer because I'm going to show you exactly the same respect you just showed me. So, you are now Bob to me, and you'll never ever change from being Bob. I don't play football for Bobby Saxton. I don't play football for Malcolm Allison. I play football for two entities – Plymouth Argyle Football Club, because they pay my wages, and I play for Barry Silkman, because I want to be the best player I can possibly be. I don't care who the manager is as long as they play me – or they can sell me. You don't know me, yet you've already made a presumption about me, so I wish you all the luck in the job and if you want to play me, play me and I'll give it my best as I always do, but did you know what, Bob? I don't really care either way."

I walked out of the office and got ready for training. The manager's office wasn't the only place that was frosty because though we trained all week, the Saturday game was called off due to heavy snow. So we trained the following week and this time the weekend game went ahead and to my surprise, Bobby picked me to start. I had an absolute blinder and we beat Sheffield Wednesday 1-0 at Hillsborough. We were back in the dressing room sitting down when Bobby did his post-match talk. He looked at me and said, "Silky, I have to say something to you. I got you completely wrong. You are nothing like I expected you to be. You were fantastic tonight and in front of all the lads, I want to apologise to you because you've completely opened my eyes. I was wrong."

I said, "Bob, not a problem," stood up to shake his hand and he gave me a hug! From there, we got along really well and there was never a problem between us again. I played in the next game against Grimsby and had another stormer, but at the next Monday training session, Bobby pulled me to one side and said, "We've got a problem. Manchester City have come in for you, and I'd already told the board I wouldn't stand in your way if anyone came in for you. The issue is, Malcolm told the board when you signed that you could only be sold for big money, so they won't let you go for a fee less than the fee he suggested. He's done this to himself!"

As it was, Malcolm came back with the money he believed I was worth, Argyle accepted the bid and after just 15 games, I was heading north for the first time in my career.

I was going to be a Manchester City player and, aged 27, this would be the biggest club of my career playing for a manager who believed in me in front of big crowds week in, week out.

What could possibly go wrong?

Chapter 6

LAW ABIDING CITYZEN

I don't think many footballers suffered as many false dawns as I did during my career – and my dream move to Manchester City looked to be over before it had started.

I took the standard medical with club doctor Norman Luft before signing the contract… and failed. To say that was a shock is an understatement because I was the fittest player I'd ever met! I was at the peak of my physicality, felt incredible and was even fitter than John Burridge, who had been a monster in training at Palace. I'd never had a knee problem in my life, yet it was my left non-kicking leg that the medical failed me on. Apparently, there was too much movement in that knee joint, but Malcolm Allison didn't believe it. He wasn't having any of it because he'd seen me train and play for the best part of three months at Plymouth and he wanted to make me a City player, so he arranged another medical – a second opinion, if you like – that he paid for himself.

The guy was a knee specialist and flew in from Belgium to do the second medical on me. Two days later, he delivered his verdict – my right knee was absolutely fine and had full movement, but my other knee, which I kicked with, was very slightly stiff, which was no great surprise but it was still a pass as far as he was concerned.

In the meantime, I had to go back to Plymouth who were obviously getting on without Barry Silkman as part of their plans. It wasn't my fault and the best solution all round seemed to be me going out on loan as it felt like I'd cut my ties there.

Luton Town came in for me, offering me a month's loan, which suited me fine as I'd be nearer home, and they had a great team and played the sort of football I enjoyed. Brian Stein, Ricky Hill, and David Moss were all top players and David Pleat was one of the best young managers in the country.

But I would only play three games for them.

The first two games went well but Pleaty wasn't at the third match for some reason. We were playing away from home and as I turned this defender, he did me with a high kick on my thigh right on half-time. I walked off towards the dressing room, I looked down and my thigh above my knee was swelling up like a balloon. In the dressing room, the physio took a look and then got me an ice pack because the swelling had got worse. He told me he didn't think I'd be going anywhere any time soon and that my night had ended.

With Pleaty absent, his assistant manager – David Coates – finished his half-time talk and then came over to me and said, "Are you going to be fit enough to go out in the second half or are you just going to lie there?"

My thigh looked terrible and it's fair to say I wasn't best pleased.

I said, "Are you serious? I'll tell you what, fuck you and fuck your club." As well as one or two other choice phrases. We travelled back to Luton, and I was fuming inside, so on the Monday morning I limped in and went and saw Pleaty.

I said, "I'm not playing for your club any more so you can piss off, Pleaty."

He asked what I was talking about, and I said, "I'm not having your assistant manager talk to me like I'm a piece of shit. I won't take that off anybody. All he had to do was come over, ask how I was doing and what was wrong because he'd have been able to see there was no way I could play on. But he came in, made himself look like a right prick in front of all the other lads and at the end of the day, who the fuck is he anyway? I'm leaving."

Pleat said, "You can't go, you've got another game to play."

I said, "I'm not playing for Luton any more." And after collecting my two pairs of boots, I left Luton Town FC and never returned.

I phoned Bobby Saxton at Plymouth to let him know I was on my way back and he said, "Well, you'll be glad to know Man City have come back in for you."

This time, there was no medical required by the club and I think the whole thing had been a ruse because City hadn't wanted to pay the original transfer fee. It didn't matter to me because I wanted to be a City player and just wanted it sorting.

Malcolm informed the chairman and the board of the results of the second medical, they went back to Plymouth, agreed a reduced transfer fee and I signed the contract – I was now finally a Manchester City player.

I'd played just 15 games for Plymouth Argyle but to this day, their fans still remember me and a few years back, I was voted by fans into the best ever Argyle XI! When I went to the dinner organised around the announcing of the team I told the packed audience that for the first 15 games of each club I played for, I was the best thing they'd ever seen. After 15 games, things went rapidly downhill!

Back to City.

I was put in a hotel in south Manchester to begin with, but I soon found a house in Didsbury that I bought, but never lived in because one of my new team-mates, Colin Viljoen, said, "Silks, what do you want to buy a house and live on your own for?"

He was right. My girlfriend had a great job in London so she wouldn't be moving north with me, but I'd already bought the property. Colin said, "Come and live with me. I've got a big, three-bed apartment near town, I'm there on my own so you can do what you want."

So I moved in with Vilj. I then sold the house I'd bought as it stood – I hadn't even redecorated – and got the same price I'd paid for it – £32,000.

The set-up at City was Tony Book as manager in name, but it was Malcolm who was running the show, and that was proving to be a problem for the club. Malcolm was selling the best players and ripping the heart out of a team that had finished runners-up and fourth in the top division in the previous three seasons.

Dave Watson, Asa Hartford, Gary Owen, Peter Barnes… the list went on so when Malcolm's wife Sally invited me over to their house in Marple for dinner, I had the chance to tell him what I thought. I'd known

Malcolm's wife Sally for many years, so that was my real connection to Malcolm.

As we finished a lovely meal, I said to Malcolm, "I think you're making a mistake. Some of these players you're selling are fantastic footballers."

He said, "Most of them are at the end of their careers, Silks."

I said, "I don't agree. They are quality internationals and if you sell players like that, you need to replace them with players who are at least as good as they are."

Malcolm said, "You've never disagreed with me before."

I said, "Well, you never asked me my opinion before. We never spoke about anything in particular at Plymouth. I've only known you for four months!"

People have always assumed I was really close to Malcolm and that we'd known each other for years, but the truth is, prior to signing for Plymouth, I knew of him but I didn't know him properly.

Malcolm said it was a little bit awkward me going round as he was the coach and I was a player, and it might look a little odd, but my friendship with Sally meant more to me than the politics of football.

He didn't take my advice very well, I've got to say, but maybe I was the only one with the big enough balls to tell him straight.

I said, "Okay, maybe you don't agree with my thinking

but let me at least tell you about one player at Crystal Palace that I saw in the youth team. They don't fancy him for some reason, but I think he's going to be a player and he'll cost you about £30,000 – his name is Steve MacKenzie and he's 17, I think."

He said, "How good is he?"

So I told him I thought he'd be in the first team within a year. He said he'd never heard of him, and I said if you go in with an offer of £20,000, you might get him.

A week or so later, Steve MacKenzie was a City player – but Malcolm had paid £250,000 for him! I asked him why he'd paid so much, and he just shrugged and said, "It's not my money." It was madness and after that, I never mentioned a player to him again. I thought, 'You know what? I don't know this guy and I don't know how he works.'

The people I got closest to at City were Mike Channon, Asa Hartford, Vilj, and Willie Donachie, who I thought a lot of.

My City debut was away to Ipswich Town where everyone thinks I scored a worldie from 35 yards – but that wasn't quite the whole story. What happened was I was running towards goal and had travelled about 20 yards when my legs turned to lead – literally like lead. So, I looked up and saw Paul Cooper, the Ipswich keeper, a good few paces off his line and decided I was going to just hit the ball as hard as I could – and I did, I leathered it, it looped upwards and over Cooper and into the net. I collapsed in a heap and as far as everyone was concerned, I'd scored a wonder goal, but it was more a shot in desperation before I fell over!

We lost that game 2-1 and a week later, I scored on my home debut at Maine Road against Wolves with a header – the only headed goal of my career at ANY level! What are the odds?

Moreover, I didn't mean to score because I'd gone to the near post to flick it on but when I turned around, it had gone through everyone and into the net.

But as much as I had enjoyed my debut, later that day, events away from football would shake me to the core with a genuine personal tragedy that I still think about more than 40 years on.

One of my closest pals was a guy called Bobby Hackett, who I'd known since I was eight or nine. He had been planning to come up and see my home debut. He lived in London, a fantastic bloke and he had a young son called Warren who went on to be a professional footballer.

During the week, Bobby had asked if I could get tickets for him and Warren to see the game, but on the Friday morning, he said, "Silks, I've decided not to come up for the Wolves game, can I come up next week against Everton instead? I reckon that will be a much better game and I'd like to bring Warren up for that one instead."

I told him it wasn't a problem and I'd sort it all out early next week.

He told me not score against Wolves and I said, "Not much fucking danger of that!"

After Wolves, I travelled back to London with my girlfriend Mandy, and I think we got off at Paddington. I got myself a late edition of the Evening Standard from one of the vendors inside the station. Under the classified results, there was a stop press section that sometimes had what was breaking news of the day or horse racing results. I noticed it said: 'Father of two, Robert Hackett, was last night stabbed to death.' My stomach turned, but I sort of dismissed it and half-convinced myself it couldn't be Bobby.

I went to a phone box and called his number, and some guy answered and all I could hear was crying in the background. I knew straight away it was Bobby who had been murdered. I said, "It's Silky, I just got off the train from Manchester…"

He straight away said Georgie, Bobby's wife, had been asking after me and asked if I would go over straight away. I did. They told me that Bobby had been in a nightclub and two guys had started arguing. Bobby got between them and told them to cool off and maybe talk about whatever the problem was. A witness said one of the men punched Bobby in the chest – only he hadn't used his fist, he'd stabbed him, and he was dead within 30 seconds.

Bobby should have been in Manchester that night and come back to London with me after the game. Now he was dead, and I'd never see him again. I just wish he'd been there instead of that nightclub.

Back at City, life had to go on, as hard as it was for some time as I felt devastated I'd lost such a good mate so tragically. I remember we played Bristol City at Maine Road in May (1980) and I was up against Norman Hunter and he told me – in no uncertain terms – that if I didn't stop taking the piss, he'd chop me in half. I said, "You'll have to catch me first." So, not long after, I started juggling the ball on the touchline and Hunter started running towards me. As he got within touching distance, I left the ball on the ground as he launched himself into a tackle, but I'd obviously seen him coming so I jumped up and over as he went underneath me, and he slid feet-first into the hoardings. He wasn't best pleased, but I just told him, "You're the one who wanted to go skiing, mate!"

Another time, I remember going to watch the younger players training and I saw a kid called Ray Ranson, who I thought looked a real prospect. I said to him afterwards, "You should be training with the first team, mate." Ray smiled, but shook his shoulders and replied,

"Actually, I've been given a free transfer and they're just trying to find me a new club and if they can't find a league club, they'll look at non-league. Nobody at City rates me as a player."

I was like, "Really? Well they've made a big mistake."

I went to see Malcolm and asked him his thoughts on Ranson, and he confirmed the club were trying to move him on. He added, "I've been told he's nowhere near good enough, Silks."

I told him whoever said that was wrong and that he was good enough for the first team now, never mind in a year or so. He listened to me this time and they kept Ray on and, when a few weeks later Kenny Clements broke his leg against Ipswich, I went to Malcolm again and said that he should give Ray a go at right-back.

He said, "Yeah, but Silks, everyone thinks he's useless."

I said, "Okay, play him once and if he is as useless as everyone says, never play him again" – so he did, and I think he went on to play more than 200 games for City over the next six years and had an unbelievable career.

My time with City, however, was about to be cut short.

After we played Crystal Palace away I stayed in London after the game until the Sunday night. Malcolm's wife Sally was pregnant and he asked if I could help her and Malcolm as they weren't getting on too well because Malcolm was giving her a lot of problems with his behaviour.

She wanted me to move in with them, at least until she had the baby, as it would hopefully calm Malcolm down.

I told her that it would look a bit odd to my teammates if I moved in with the manager and his wife! She said I'd be doing it for her over anyone else and as we'd been friends for a long time, I thought that I had to help out in whatever way I could. For me, it was always people first and I thought to myself, if I can't help her in her hour of need, who was I anyway?

I had to help, so I moved in with the Allisons. I told the lads what I was doing and that it was just for a short time because I didn't want them to find out from somebody else. I explained why I was doing it, and they all accepted it. I'm not sure what they thought of it privately, because it was a bizarre situation, but I didn't care. I was helping an old friend out and that was the bottom line.

I'd been there a couple of weeks, Sally had the baby, and everything seemed to be going well, but after the game I mentioned earlier against Palace, misguided loyalty to Malcolm inadvertently led to my own downfall.

We'd been beaten 2-0 at Selhurst Park and I remember former England manager Ron Greenwood had named me as Man of the Match on the BBC's radio coverage, so I was pleased that I'd given a good showing against my old club. I won a bottle of champagne – which I gave away as I didn't drink the stuff – and stayed with my girlfriend Mandy in London over the weekend and was back at Platt Lane for training on the Monday morning.

Malcolm wasn't at training, but that wasn't completely unheard of if he had business to attend to or whatever. But then Tony Book had asked me where Malcolm was, and as I didn't know what to say, I told him he'd said he would be back in on Tuesday or Wednesday. I headed back to Marple in the early afternoon and when I arrived, I said, "Sal, where's Malcolm?" I hadn't seen him, at least not since the game – but neither had Sally! He hadn't travelled back after the match. My first instinct was that he was on a bender in London somewhere, so I spent most of Monday evening trying to track him down via his friends in London, but nobody knew where he was. He'd completely disappeared off the radar and I started to wonder if he'd done a Lord Lucan!

On Tuesday morning at training, I had to lie to Tony again and said Malcolm was ill in bed with flu and that the local doctor would go and see him. After training, the chairman Peter Swales walked across to see me and said, "Where is Malcolm?" I told him what I told Tony, and he said, "Okay, I'm coming around to his house this afternoon to see him."

Now I had a big problem because Malcolm, of course, wasn't there! I said to Sally that when the chairman's green Jaguar appeared, she'd need to have the baby make a fuss in the background and I'd handle the rest. I put the chain on and when he arrived, Sally started tickling the baby who was laughing away but it sounded a bit like crying as well. Peter Swales knocked on the door and I opened it a little. He said, "I want to see Malcolm. Now."

I said that he couldn't because Malcolm had a really bad virus that Sally and the baby also now had. He asked me how come I didn't have it and I told him that because I was living there, I must be immune to it or something. He asked me the doctor's name that Malcolm had been seeing so I gave him the name of his doctor in Marple. I then had to call him to warn him, and he told me he couldn't give information out anyway because of patient confidentiality.

Swales visited the surgery, and the doctor told him he was sorry, but he couldn't help. He must have been furious and probably suspected that Malcolm was up to no good somewhere when he was meant to be managing his football club. He knew Malcolm very well and he didn't like being made a fool of. The trouble was, I was now an accessory to the crime, and I knew I'd have to pay the price at some stage.

It was even more tense because we were playing

Manchester United at the weekend and at Wednesday training, Tony came up and asked how Malcolm was, so I said, "A bit better." I was just praying I'd find him in time for the Manchester derby. Tony said he was unsure what team to select on Saturday, and I just said that Malcolm had mentioned to start with the team that finished the game against Palace.

We went through patterns of play, set-piece drills and game prep and as I left, Tony said that he hoped Malcolm would be back in for Thursday and I just smiled and said, "Yeah, so do I!"

When I got back I said to Sally that we needed to find him, and fast. Then it clicked. I said, "You know where I'm going wrong? I'm asking people at nightclubs if Malcolm is there. What I need to do is say that I know he is there! So the first club I called, they said that he wasn't there. For the second one – Tramps – I asked the girl who answered if I could talk with Malcolm. She asked, "Malcolm who?" I said "Malcolm Allison" and she told me she'd go and fetch him. Finally!

Malcolm came on the phone, and I asked him what he was playing at? He said, "Hello Silks, how are you?" I was a little industrial with my language and he just told me not to worry and that he'd be arriving at Piccadilly Station just after 9am the next day and that I should pick him up.

So I did. I met him on the platform and immediately

saw he was wearing the suit – shirt, trousers, shoes, the lot – that he'd had on the last time I'd seen him! His jacket was all creased and his tie was scrunched up so I said he should put them in the boot of my car and just go in wearing the shirt and trousers he had on because nobody else would recall what he'd been wearing nearly a week ago. He told me he owed me his life for protecting him and looking after his family.

I went into training on Friday relieved it was all over. The session went well, and I was looking forward to playing in my first Manchester derby the following day.

We trained at Maine Road in preparation, and everything seemed normal, as the plan had been to start with the same XI that had finished the game against Palace, but after the session we were told to wait until the team sheets went up in the dressing room, which was really unusual. As far as I was concerned, I was a shoo-in to start the game, especially as I'd got Man of the Match in our last match. At least, that's what I thought.

The chairman then appeared and said to Malcolm he wanted a word in his office, and he said, "No problem, Mr Chairman," and walked out. Not long after, Tony Book pinned the starting eleven and sub to the board and I had no intentions of bothering to look at it and as I made to leave I said, "Boys, see you all tomorrow," Asa Hartford said, "Silks, you'd best come and look at this."

I walked over and saw that not only was my name not anywhere to be seen and would not be starting against Manchester United, I was also down as the 14th man for the reserves game against United reserves at Old Trafford in the morning – as low as I could possibly be for our second XI! I couldn't figure it out. I headed back to Marple to hear Malcolm's version of events, but he stayed at a hotel in Manchester and didn't come home.

I later discovered what had happened. Malcolm had told Tony Book and Peter Swales that he'd just needed some time to himself and that he'd had to get away from everyone and everything for a while. All that time, I'd been covering for him because nobody had seen him for a few days, just to buy him some time and what had he done in return? He'd completely thrown me under the bus and then got in the driver's seat and reversed it back over me! Peter Swales needed a sacrificial lamb and focused solely on my role in the whole mess. He wasn't going to take Malcolm on, but someone had to pay, and he said: "Right, Silkman's out. He's a fucking liar!" In his eyes, he'd been made a fool of and even though everything I'd done had been to protect Malcolm. In his eyes, I'd committed the bigger crime by being deceitful towards him.

Peter Swales called me personally to tell me I wouldn't be playing for City again.

He said, "Just to let you know, you're down for the

reserves tomorrow but after that, you are banned from Manchester City Football Club. I'll find a club for you, but I never ever want to see you at the club again."

I couldn't believe it.

I'd only played 21 games for City, and I loved my time there. I felt I hadn't done anything wrong, but in hindsight, I should have just got on with my football and left Malcolm to fight his own battles.

It was too late for that, however. There was nothing I could do. It would be many, many years before I would speak to Malcolm again and even then it was only after an apology. I heard later Sally finished with Malcolm not long after I had been told I was finished at City because she just couldn't forgive him.

What a mess.

Chapter 7

THE ISRAELITE

As I was contemplating life after Manchester City, I was contacted by an Israeli sports journalist called Pini Zahavi. He had brokered a move for Israeli international Avi Cohen to move from Maccabi Tel Aviv to Liverpool and was well connected throughout Europe. He told me he wanted to take me to Maccabi Tel Aviv so I agreed to meet him, and we spoke at length where he explained he planned to take me on loan until the end of the season and why he thought it would be a great move for me.

There was nothing else on the table at that moment and the opportunity of playing under the hot sun appealed to me, so I decided to go and find out what it was like. The initial plan was to spend a week or so out there, take in the training sessions and see how it all felt, and when I arrived I met the manager who was a great guy called Nassim Bahir. He was a proper football man who knew a lot about the game, a lot about me and he knew how I played and where I might fit into his team, which impressed me no end.

The training was terrific – I loved it – and after a week, I returned to London and informed Pini I would join Maccabi. I had to get one or two things in order before I left, so arranged to return in a week's time. I was soon all set for a new adventure and flew out to Tel Aviv as planned, taking Mandy and my dad out with me. But when I arrived at the club to sign various documents, the manager I'd got on so well with had gone and a new guy had taken over – and he was clueless! It had happened yet again! If managers knew of the jinx I seemed to be and that so many had left the clubs they'd just signed me to play for, I doubt anyone would have signed me again.

After one training session under the new guy, Zvi Rosen, I knew I'd made a huge mistake because we played basketball for two hours and didn't kick a ball once!

I'm five foot eight so it's fair to say basketball wasn't one of my strengths! However, I'd agreed a deal and was stuck for the time being.

It was winter there, but still pleasant and sunny and

Tel Aviv was an interesting city so I decided to try and make the best of it until the end of the season, but I wouldn't quite make it that far, thanks to an incident that was difficult to believe.

We used to meet as a team at the Maccabi Tel Aviv club house, which was on the beachfront facing the sea. Every Friday, we'd go over the team for the next game and the tactics – not that I could understand a word as it was all in Hebrew, but at least I knew roughly what I was being asked to do as they had a board with magnetic initials on and 'BS' was definitely involved.

Meanwhile, Pini had asked me if it was true that I had a great singing voice and featured on other people's records? I told him it was, and he was amazed and said there was a big festival on, and asked if I would like to go and rehearse at a restaurant in Jerusalem – and maybe even sing to some people?

I thought 'why not?' My first attempt to reach the venue had to be abandoned because although it was 23 degrees in Tel Aviv, the road to Jerusalem, which was about an hour's drive away, was closed due to a heavy snowfall! You couldn't make it up.

So, the next morning, once training had finished, I got a lift to the restaurant, with everywhere still covered in snow, had a sing on the stage with the band and sang five or six songs, not realising the festival organisers were among those gathered. After I'd finished, they came over to me and insisted I sang at the upcoming festival. And I did, performing to around 3,500 people – and got great reviews in the paper the next day, so I was told.

Back at the club, it was hard going with no interpreter, but a few of the lads spoke some English and helped explain what the coach was saying. In the beginning, it was a bit of a disaster, but gradually I understood my role better and my team-mates learned how I played, and things started to improve. For a time, it was enjoyable but there was trouble ahead.

And when I was asked to play for the Israeli national team, little did I realise I was also about to sign up for a spell in the military – not that anyone told me! I was asked if I would become an Israeli national and play international football and, at that stage of my career, it was quite a compliment. I had to get an Israeli passport, which you could only do if you have been in the country for two years. I'd been there a month at best – but they fast-tracked me a passport so I could play. Friends in high places!

I played in a friendly for Israel against Everton and was available for their next game, if called upon.

My new passport had arrived with a green card with Israeli writing on it, so I asked a lady who lived in the apartment next door and spoke good English what exactly it said. She took a look and casually said, "Oh, that's the form you need to fill out to go into the army."

Come again? I might have misheard that!

I was a footballer, not a soldier, and when I asked officials at the club to explain it better, they told me I'd need to do three years' national service, but if there was a war, I shouldn't worry because I'd be on the second line, not the front! Apparently, all I needed to do was go in and take the troops physical training three or four times a week.

Corporal Silkman at your service – only I wouldn't be in the country long enough to fight in the trenches as what was an unbelievable week was about to take an ever more surreal turn.

On Saturdays, ahead of a home game, we used to meet at 12.30 at the club house, then pile into each other's cars and head to the stadium for a 3pm kick-off. That was a routine we stuck to rigidly, and so for this particular home game, I went to see Mandy and my dad on the beach before heading the half-mile or so to the club house.

It was a scorching day, and I decided to walk to training – something I did regularly as I had no car over there – and after telling my dad and girlfriend that the tickets would be waiting for them on the door at the stadium, I checked my watch and it was 12.20, so I was bang on track for the pre-match meeting.

As I approached the club house, I could sense something wasn't quite right. There were no players milling around outside, nobody sat on the steps, and I couldn't figure out why. I asked a lady passing by if I could check the time with her and her watch said the same as mine – 12.25. So I continued to the club house and found the doors closed, but I could hear talking inside, so I pushed them open and there were the rest of the lads, who all stopped and looked around at me.

A number of them pointed to their watches and I looked up at the huge clock on the wall which said 12.26, so I couldn't understand what the issue was. I looked over at the magnetic board and my initials were no longer there, with another guy's initials in my position. I sat down, waited for the meeting to end and then one of the lads asked why I'd been so late. I said I wasn't late!

I walked out of the room and the manager came over to me and said, "What are you doing? You have killed me and now you can't play." I asked what he was talking about, and he said that the meeting was at 12, not 12.30, and as I'd been half-an-hour late, he'd had to leave me out. "That's what we do for a 2.30pm kick-off."

Finally, I knew. I said, "Well how would I know that?"

He said, "Because I told everyone last night at the meeting..." Then he added, "Oh no! I told everyone in Hebrew."

I nodded. "Exactly. How the fuck was I supposed to know? That's why I turned up at the time we normally meet at."

"This is a disaster," he said. "I'll tell you what I will do. You are on the bench, so I will take your replacement off after five minutes and bring you on."

"You can't do that!"

"20 minutes then?"

"No," I protested. And now I didn't trust him because I thought that if I was sub, he'd bring me on at the first opportunity and the players will think I'd engineered it all and that I was an absolute arsehole. I asked how many players he had, and he said 14, so I said, "Here's what we will do. I'll go home and you say I was ill with the flu, then nobody will have a problem, and he agreed it was a good idea. I wished the lads good luck and headed back to the beach to explain what had happened to Mandy and my dad. I then headed back to the apartment and around five o'clock, the phone rang, and it was Pini.

"Silky," he said, "what are you doing to me? We've drawn 0-0 against the bottom side and everyone is asking why you weren't playing. So the manager said that they'd found you asleep on the beach!"

I couldn't believe it. I told Pini the truth and to go and ask the players what had really happened, which he did, and he later confirmed everything I'd told him was true. For me, however, that was the end of it. I told Pini I needed to get away and that I wouldn't be playing for Maccabi Tel Aviv again.

My new Israeli passport meant I needed permission to leave the country, so I told the authorities my mum was ill in order to get a pass out. I booked a flight home to London for Sunday morning, and to avoid a big fuss, told my dad and Mandy to fly home later on Sunday evening. I was soon on the plane and heading home and my time with Maccabi was over.

I also couldn't return to Israel in case they threw me in the army when I touched down, so I had to go through a process of denouncing my Israeli citizenship and give up my passport as well.

In my short time in the country, I'd been the capital team's star footballer, become an Israeli citizen and international player, a festival singer of some repute and an army conscript – not to mention becoming the first ever European jew to play in the country and the first professional footballer from England to play there.

It had been an amazing experience, but not one that I wanted to repeat any time soon.

No wonder it would be almost 25 years before I eventually did return to Israel, and I was still relieved I wasn't greeted by the military police.

At the time, I was thinking I'll write a book about this one day!

THE ISRAELITE

In fact, my whole career up to that point has been the stuff of fiction that you literally couldn't make up.

Still, I was home again and, fortunately, it wasn't long before I was playing football again, though it wouldn't be the last time that Pini Zahavi and me worked together…

Chapter 8

THE BEES' KNEES

I hadn't been home long before Brentford offered me the chance of a short-term deal on the understanding that if a better opportunity came up, they'd let me go.

Fred Callaghan, the manager, had told his chairman that he thought he had a chance of signing me, that he thought I was a fantastic player, but that I didn't see my long-term future there, and he explained that if I was signed, it should be on the premise that if a bigger club came in for me they wouldn't stand in my way. The chairman sanctioned the deal on that basis and then contacted City, who I was still contracted to.

Bernard Halford, the City secretary, called me and asked if I wanted to go and speak to Fred at Brentford. I knew Fred from my time at Fulham where he'd been a full-back. He later told me he had followed my career closely and was enthusiastic about working with me.

Fred said, "Silky, I'd love you to come and play for me – you probably won't be here longer than three or four months, but I'd love you to come and play for us – but do you want to come? I've agreed a deal with Man City and if anyone comes in for you, we won't stand in your way."

How could I argue with those terms? I told him I'd be more than happy to accept his offer and so I signed for Brentford a few days later.

I went to see Fred in his office about one or two things and as I came out, a builder was coming up the stairs. He was covered in dust and looked like he'd been working on one of the projects at Griffin Park, so I directed him to where Fred was and then headed into the dressing rooms for morning training.

About 15 minutes later, Fred comes in with this builder and says, "I'd like to introduce you to our new signing."

We all thought he was having a wind-up, but it turned out to be Terry Hurlock, who had been playing non-league football for a while and labouring on a building site in between.

It turned out he'd been at West Ham as a kid but

because he was skinny, they let him go because they thought he'd never make it. He decided to keep playing, but also build himself up physically and to do that, he thought labouring on a building site was the best way. What a player he turned out to be!

We also had Stan Bowles and Chris Kamara, so there was a great mix of flair backed with steel and I loved my time with the club.

I was enjoying my football again and though I don't remember that much of the games I played, other people – fans and team-mates – would often ask me in later years whether I remembered doing this or remembered doing that, but I honestly don't.

The only thing that I can't forget is something that still makes me laugh out loud today.

Around that time, there was a Bob Hope film out called *Son of Paleface*, and in it there was a scene where Painless Potter – Hope's character – believed he was a sharpshooter and the fastest gun in the west. It was Jane Russell's character who was actually doing the shooting in the film, though Hope didn't know it as he couldn't have shot a barn door from six yards.

Whenever Hope had a gunfight, Russell would hide and do the shooting for him.

Back to the scene in question and Hope is in a saloon where a notorious gun slinger is outside waiting for him.

As he's leaving the bar to go and take him on, a guy

stops him and says, "I know this guy – when he goes to shoot, he crouches down, so stand on your toes." Then he is stopped by another cowboy who says, "When he leans to the left, he shoots to the right." He takes it on board and reminds himself of the advice.

Then he gets stopped again and this guy says, "If the sun's in the east, make sure you come from the west." Hope is reminding himself when he's stopped again by another passer-by who says, "When the wind's in the north, he'll aim to the south."

By the time he gets to the shootout spot, he's mumbling, "If he stands on his tiptoes crouch down, and if shoots from the west with the sun in the east and the wind…"

It was hilarious and one of the funniest scenes I'd ever seen.

Most of the lads had seen it so ahead of our game against Fulham, Fred took training as usual and gathered us all in to tell us about what to expect. He looked at our centre-halves and said, "They've only got one outstanding player up front – Tony Mahoney – but he's only got one trick. He'll come at you, but when he leans to the left, he'll go to the right."

We had a striker called Tony Funnell and he immediately said, "And when he crouches down low, stand on your toes and when the wind's in the east, he'll run to the west."

The lads fell about laughing, but Fred was apoplectic

and shouted, "Get back in the fucking dressing room! You're not playing tomorrow!"

And he dropped him! By the following week, he'd gone completely – Fred had kicked him out for good, but he's still responsible for the funniest thing I ever saw in my career.

About three months into my time with the Bees, Crystal Palace's chief scout, Arnie Warren, called me to see if I would meet him and somebody else at a hotel in the centre of London. I went along and there was Terry Venables sitting with Arnie who said, "How do you fancy signing for QPR?"

I said, "Fuck me, I'd love to!"

He said, "Silks, I've just got the job, and I want you to come and play for me, but I can't sign you until next week so tell Fred you've picked up a knock and can't play this weekend."

QPR were a club that suited my style as they'd always been a team who liked to play good football, and it would be good to play for TV again so I said I would sign.

At the next training session, I went up to Fred and said, "Fred, I can't play, I've got an injury..."

He just laughed and said, "Silks, I know you're not injured. Terry has come in for you and we've spoken. It's all good, you stay at home this weekend and then you'll go to QPR next week and sign with our blessing as agreed."

Brentford were as good as their word and so as soon as Terry Venables got the job at QPR, he made me his first signing.

Chapter 9

SPAGHETTI HOOPS

Terry Venables had sold the whole deal to me, but I really didn't need convincing.

He told me about the players QPR had and how they were going to play, and he said he thought I'd be perfect for the club, and I agreed. What I didn't know was he'd spoken to the QPR captain, Glenn Roeder, asking if he knew me or not.

"Silky? Yeah, I know him," Glenn said.

TV said, "Good, he'll take us up the league on his own, not just because of his ability, but because of his character. He's got an infectious personality that will rub off on everyone and energise us because everyone is walking around with a long face, feeling sorry for themselves and I want a player who will turn this club around and I think Silky is that man."

Glenn told me that many years later. It was quite a compliment from one of the best and most innovative managers English football had ever seen.

So, I signed for QPR who were struggling near the bottom of what is now the Championship and after I made my debut, we went on an unbeaten run of 13 games and climbed up to sixth. That first game was away to Grimsby Town on a freezing Saturday afternoon, and in a game fitting of the occasion, we drew 0-0 at Blundell Park, but that was the start of that great run. If you can do it on a sub-zero Saturday in Grimsby, you can do it anywhere – as the saying goes!

There was a great group of lads at QPR, and it was a happy time for me.

I always say the best player I ever played against was Glenn Hoddle, but the best player I ever played with in my life was Tony Currie. He was a different class – a Rolls Royce of a footballer who I would have paid to watch. It was a genuine pleasure to play in the same team as a player as gifted as he was and he should have won triple the amount of England caps he did – 17, I believe. We also had Glenn (Roeder), Steve Wicks,

Terry Fenwick, Andy King, Don Shanks... The fans were brilliant with me and I was able to express myself and do my thing in a team that wanted to play attractive, attacking football.

I was all about dribbling, speed and passing – I must have made two tackles in my whole career! I just wanted to play football the way it should be played and was always looking to attack and go forward. In today's market I reckon I'd have fetched a fair few quid because hardly anybody tackles anyone any more and there's only one or two that want everyone to run around like chickens with no heads from start to finish.

That doesn't mean I didn't have a good work ethic. In a pre-season friendly for QPR, TV asked me to wear a tracking device to see how much running I was doing during 90 minutes and also to play in central midfield. Most players today average around eight to nine miles, but in that game – which was a fairly typical game for me – I ran 13.2 miles. I could run all day and, as I'd been told as a youngster, football was all about finding space, whether that was running into space or staying put and letting others run around you and still finding space, just as Eric Cantona and Teddy Sheringham used to do so well.

I was able to continue my music career as well as TV was more than happy for me to keep singing, just as he had been at Crystal Palace. I was doing a lot of backing vocals for Mickie Most, who was one of the biggest and best music producers of the day. He'd become a household name, partly because he featured on an ITV programme called New Faces where he was a panellist judging new musical acts. He was the prototype that Simon Cowell became. He had Hot Chocolate, Suzi Quatro, Racey, The Animals, Lulu, and a load of other top acts in his stable, so I was always in work earning a few extra quid.

I did some vocals on one of Hot Chocolate's biggest UK hits, 'No Doubt About It' alongside Errol Brown, the lead singer, as well as doing a load of demo vocals to see how songs sounded. But I never thought I was any good at backing vocals as it wasn't my strength, where as a lead vocal I could sing in three different keys and turn my hand to any style. I just wasn't that good on harmonies, no matter how hard I practised.

In fact, Mickie organised the QPR squad to record a version of 'Singin' the Blues' as a theme for the team to run out to.

As we began the first attempt, Mickie would keep stopping us to pick out individuals who were tone deaf! With no autotune in those days, some of the lads were painfully bad and while you couldn't make someone who sounded shit sound good, you could make someone who was good sound terrific.

In the end, Mickie said, "Silks, I think we should

just do it with you and treble or quadruple your vocals because the others can't sing a note."

Around this time, all the record companies in London were having a five-a-side tournament for charity and Mickie had put together a team of singers and celebrities together for his Rak label. He asked me and I told him I'd love to be involved. I got wind that Genesis star Phil Collins would be playing – somebody I'd always wanted to meet. On the day of the game, we were warming up and I asked Mickie if he could introduce me to Phil.

I saw Mickie next to this small guy who was losing his hair and he called me across. "Silks, Phil Collins; Phil Collins, this is Silks," he said.

The guy put his hand out to shake mine saying, "Nice to meet you, Silks." I said to him and Mickie, "Yeah, right – this is Phil Collins."

I was looking around for some six-foot, good looking drummer from one of the world's biggest bands, so I had no idea who the guy was I'd just been introduced to.

I went over to my mate Carl Douglas, who'd had a massive hit with 'Kung Fu Fighting', and I said, "Who is that standing with Mickie?"

He said, "Are you taking the piss, Silks? That's Phil Collins!"

Oh Shit.

I walked back over to Phil, held my hand out and said, "Hi Phil, sorry about that," but he just turned his back to me.

We didn't become close friends after that!

I was doing a lot of session work and singing in a few nightclubs as well.

I sang every week at the nightclub in Lambeth near the Elephant & Castle owned by Joey Pyle and Charlie Kray, a couple of notorious London gangsters.

Charlie, as you've probably worked out, was the brother of Ronnie and Reggie Kray, and that was something I did for several years and also led to me making some close associations with people you didn't want to mess with. Singing was my passion and I still held hopes of making it as a singer and being able to leave football behind – that was how much it meant to me and how much I loved doing it.

Life was good though. I was very happy at Loftus Road, we finished eighth in the second tier and were confident of really giving it a go in the 1981/82 season… only I wouldn't be part of it because I upset TV and was on my travels again.

The reason?

There was a move to install artificial pitches in England and QPR announced that they would be installing one. I knew TV had links with the company laying the pitches and that he would get a commission for each one installed that would run into several thousand pounds I would imagine. But as I always did, I spoke out when I thought something was wrong and I thought laying a plastic pitch was a big mistake – and said as much during an interview to a journalist.

The thing was, for me, it couldn't have been better because of the way I played and the fact that I wouldn't ever be tackled on those sort of pitches unless somebody wanted a nasty carpet burn down their thigh. It was called Omni Turf and was basically a big green carpet rolled over a concrete base with a layer of sand in between, so you can imagine it was like playing on a car park. But I knew it wasn't right for everyone and said that I thought it would end Tony Currie's career because the hard surface would affect his ankles and knees because Tony and a few others were already struggling with various wear and tear injuries.

Maybe I should have kept my mouth shut and things would have carried on the way they had, but TV took great offence to what I'd said, because I was going against his validation and, more likely, because he'd make less money if fewer pitches were laid. In the interview, for a football magazine, I also said that I doubted that more than five or six clubs would have plastic pitches and the ones that did would rip them up and go back to grass within a couple of years.

TV got the right hump, but I was proved right on

a number of levels. It did end Tony Currie's career because after one season on plastic, he barely played again. But that wasn't the only reason I left QPR. TV had promised me a substantial rise if I had a good first season and as I finished runner-up in the players' player of the year award and in the top three for the fans' player of the year, I knew I'd done my bit.

So, in the close season, I went to see TV to ask for the raise he'd promised me – but he wouldn't give it to me. I had commitments to meet, had bought a new house on the strength of that promised wage increase, but he wouldn't budge.

I said, "TV, you've fucked me here. You made a promise and now you're telling me you're not going to pay me what you said?"

He asked me what I intended to do, and I said I would have to move.

I said, "You've given me no option. I don't want to move because I don't think I'll get a better club. We've got a great team, great players and I love it here, but now I have to move on because I need that rise and you've fucked me. I don't fucking get it, TV."

I still think he was just getting back at me because of what I'd said about plastic pitches, but he was pretty blasé about it all and just said, "Okay, fine, there are six or seven clubs that want you but only one is London – Leyton Orient."

Orient were in the same division as QPR, less glamorous with smaller crowds, but I felt my bridges had been burned – for me and not by me – at QPR.

And while Orient didn't particularly excite me, I was happy to at least talk with them, so I went along to meet the chairman Brian Winston – a lovely man – who told me he'd give me more than I'd been earning at QPR plus a decent signing-on fee.

I was convinced, but for the first time in my career, I was making a move because of money and not much else.

A contract was drawn up, I said my goodbyes to the QPR players and staff who couldn't figure out why I was being allowed to leave, and I signed for Leyton Orient.

Was it the right move for me? No. If I'm honest, it was a shit move career-wise, but I had bills to pay and wanted to stay in London, so I needed to make the best of it. It was a case of 'Brisbane Road, here I come'.

Chapter 10

THE ORIENT EXPRESS

When I signed for Leyton Orient, their manager was Jimmy Bloomfield, but he was sacked without me ever playing a game under him and Paul Went had taken over. I'd honestly lost track of the number of managers who had fallen under 'The Curse of Silks' – it was incredible. Signing me seemed to be the kiss of death!

I think Paul had 21 days in charge before Ken Knighton took over, so within three months I'd had three different managers, which didn't bode well for the club's fortunes.

The first game Orient had played after I signed came

too soon for me to take part, so I watched from the directors' box as I hadn't even trained with the squad yet. As the game progressed, the realisation sank in that I might have made a big mistake. They were dreadful, just awful to watch and already had the look of a side who were a nailed on certainty for relegation.

I remember thinking, 'Oh my God, what have I done?' Don't get me wrong – they were a great bunch of lads, but just completely lacking in confidence.

I'd left the likes of Tony Currie and Simon Stainrod behind at a club I loved for this lot?

By the end of the 90 minutes, I was cursing myself that I hadn't looked into the move properly. I'd taken the first offer that came along and now I'd made my bed and would have to lie in it. I honestly couldn't see any positives from the game I'd just seen and though he was only in his third week, the chairman had already seen enough and Went went! Sacked after three weeks.

So Ken Knighton was already Orient's third manager of the season. Stan Bowles had also moved to Orient from Nottingham Forest for a six-figure sum, but we soon learned that Knighton's idea of playing football was not Stan's idea of playing football and definitely not mine, either.

One of our first meetings with the new manager left Stan and I shaking our heads. We'd both been in the game a long time and could see where this was all heading.

Knighton said, "Some people say keep the ball and dominate possession; others say make as many chances as possible and score lots of goals – I say, give them rocks. Fucking kick them and let them know you're there. That's what I want from my team."

Shit. Had it really come to this? 'Give them rocks' for fuck's sake.

Stan and I probably hadn't reached double figures for tackling in our careers – and that's combined – so we weren't going to be kicking rocks out of anyone any time soon. It wasn't long before Knighton targeted Stan, a wonderful, skilful footballer – albeit at the wrong end of his career – who could have just sat in the middle of the park, spraying passes, and controlling games had he been used correctly. A parting of the ways was inevitable, and early on in one particular game, Knighton was lambasting Stan for not tracking back and Stan just looked over at him and smiled. Then he walked off the pitch with the game still going on, shouting, "I'm not fucking playing for you any more, pal."

That was that. Stan left Orient and later signed for Brentford.

I had some great times with Stan over the years and while it was true – as Manchester City manager Joe Mercer once said – that if he could pass a betting shop as well as he passed a football he'd have been one of the best players this country had ever seen, he was still a great lad. We used to go along to White City and watch the greyhounds on a regular basis, even though I wasn't a particularly big gambler. Often on a Saturday night, there'd be me, Stan, Don Shanks, and Alan Hudson, and because of the era we could move about without too much fuss. Can you imagine four top players doing that today? We were all creative footballers in a time when there was a lot of frustration because of the way football was played back then and the pitches we had to play on, so we needed to be creative in other ways. While I had my singing to keep me sane, Stan loved to gamble and drink, much to his own detriment.

Most managers didn't know how to use skilful players to their best ability, unless you were lucky enough to have someone like Terry Venables in charge. TV was so far ahead of his time, and I find it remarkable that people think that a high press is something that's just been invented, because TV was doing that at Crystal Palace back in 1976 – he called it 'closing down from the front'.

TV said, "In years to come, other teams will play the way we are, but they will adapt it and call it something different to look as though it's a new way of playing – but it will be exactly the same as what we're doing now."

Of course, he was spot on.

He was the most creative and innovative coach I ever came across – he thought, acted, and operated differently and was years ahead of his time. I remember he told me once, "One day, Silks, managers will earn more than the players because clubs will realise just how important they are."

My response was, "Fuck me, TV – I bet that's a long, long way away."

He just smiled and said, "Well, however long away it is, Silks, it's going to happen."

And of course, it did.

I carried all that info and wisdom I'd learned from people like Terry with me in my career and used it whenever I could.

I still can't believe I didn't move on and have one last go at a better club that played football the way I wanted to.

I stayed with Orient for four years and most of it was pretty uneventful and not enjoyable as far as I was concerned.

That first season in 1981/82 ended in relegation, so I'd gone from playing in an attractive team pushing for promotion to the top flight with QPR to the third tier of English football in the space of a few months.

Knighton was a really nice guy, but he was a useless manager.

Tactically, he didn't have a clue. His training methods

were poor, and his team selection was bizarre. It got so bad that towards the end of that first season, I refused to play. He'd left me out for a few games, and I'd had enough, so when he said I'd be playing in a must-win game away to Norwich City, I said, "Ken, I'm not playing for you. This is shit and I've had enough."

He played a lad called Smith in midfield for that game, and, as cruel as it sounds, he has to be one of the worst footballers I've ever seen – he was so bad, it was scary. His dad was something to do with the club's hierarchy.

The other lads were asking me to play, so I did, but we were as good as down anyway and we still lost 2-0.

I was picked for the final game of the season against Sheffield Wednesday who could still get promoted if results went their way and they must have thought they just had to turn up to roll us over because we had been so shit for so long.

As far as I was concerned, this would be my last game for the club, so I decided I'd do things my way for that game.

We absolutely battered Wednesday that day, beating them 4-0 at Brisbane Road and Knighton was furious afterwards. He was hammering us for being so shit all season when we had clearly had the ability to do much better, but it was down to his management and tactics.

THE ORIENT EXPRESS

He went around the dressing room, until he came to John Margerrison, and he stopped and turned around to the rest of the group and said: "This guy epitomises what football is all about – he's never stopped running, unlike some of you. He's never stopped trying, unlike some of you – these are the players you need at your football club," then, looking it at me, "not the skilled forwards and fancy Dans – if you don't have John Margerrisons in your team, you're fucked!"

Then, on the following Monday, he went and gave John Margerrison a free transfer! That's what I had to deal with at Orient.

I remember being at the club when Marge went in to see Ken and he said, "Silks, I'm going in to get a new contract and I need £100 a week more than I'm on now."

I said, "Marge, you've no chance of getting that because we've just been relegated – how are you going to get a rise?"

"Don't worry, Silks, I'll get it."

Ten minutes later he came out and said, "Silks, he's fucking let me go."

I honestly didn't know whether to laugh or not, because of the way he'd been with him on the Saturday, so I said, "He's what?"

He said, "He just told me I'd had a great season, but he wasn't keeping me." And off he went. Unbelievable.

Next, it was my turn to go in and see Ken, so I went in and said, "Well if you're not keeping Marge, you're definitely not keeping me."

He just looked up and said, "You're right. I'm not."

"Ken," I said, "you're a lovely bloke, but you haven't got a fucking clue about football and trust me when I tell you my knowledge of football is better than anyone you'll ever meet in your life. When Terry Venables asks you for advice and tells me I'm the best judge of a player he's ever met, I would rather believe him than believe you."

I walked out and felt relieved it was all over. Or so I thought.

A few days later, the Orient assistant manager Frank Clark, who was an absolutely brilliant person, called me and said, "Silks, have you signed for anyone yet?" I told him I hadn't – yet. He said, "Come and be my player/assistant manager."

I asked at which club, and he said, "Leyton Orient – Knighton's just been sacked, and they want me to take over."

I paused for a moment and then said, "Franko, I'll be there."

The problem we had at Orient was simple. There was no money, no investment and we couldn't pay decent wages.

Frank trusted my instinct and was relying on me to

find talent that cost next to nothing – that was part of my remit.

So I got to work, doing what I believed I did best – finding talent that had maybe slipped under the radar and at Orient, they'd have to be well off the radar for the peanuts we could afford to pay, but there are always ways if you can be a little creative. You need to have your ear to the ground and be on the lookout continually, and always be willing to take a punt if the right opportunity comes along.

Case in point, I was in a betting shop one day in Sudbury, and there was a guy in there who knew me and said, "There's a really good player who is playing for Wembley at the moment, Silks – you should take a look."

I said, "Really? Where's their home ground?" It turned out it was at the back of the shop I was in!

He insisted I come and watch this guy and so I asked when he was next likely to play – the answer was the next day, as they had a midweek home game. I told Frank Clark I was going to go and watch this 21-year-old kid play who had just joined Wembley and I arrived at 19.45, in time for kick-off. It was close to where I lived, and after 15 minutes, I left and went home to call Frank.

He asked why I was home so early. I told him I'd already seen enough. "We've got to sign him." He asked why I was so sure. I said, "Because I just saw him do one thing that none of the forwards we've got are capable of doing and I don't need to see any more. We've got to sign him."

Frank said that was good enough for him and told me to do the deal. I managed to get the lad's number and it turned out he was fitting double-glazing windows. He'd been at Fulham as a kid, it hadn't worked out and he was happy doing his job and playing non-league football.

Him and his dad came around to my house a day later and it took me two hours to convince him. I said, "Come along to one training session. If you don't like it, you can stay doing what you're doing and never come back again, but if you do like it, then sign for Leyton Orient."

The following week he came to training, and I said to Frank, "Put a game on and watch how good he is." We had a centre-half who used to be at Crystal Palace called Tommy Cunningham and I said to Tommy, "Mark him and see how good he is." After 20 minutes, Tommy shouted over, "I can't fucking live with him!" He'd been turned inside out, and Frank just smiled. I said, "We've got to sign him today." And we did. He was earning £120 per week for Wembley and his double-glazing, so we gave him £200 per week, plus appearance and goal money and he would go on to have a really good career.

THE ORIENT EXPRESS

His name? Richard Cadette. Richard went on to play for Sheffield United, Brentford, Millwall, Southend United and Falkirk and it had all come from that off-chance chat in a betting shop.

Around this time I took part in a charity game – a proper, competitive match featuring pros, some recently retired pros and several non-league players. It wasn't an arty-farty showbiz game where everyone fucks around, but a fundraiser with an edge to it.

I went along and played the full 90 minutes and as I came off the pitch, Spurs legend Steve Perryman came over and said, "Silks, you've just been paid a massive compliment. Ossie Ardiles wants to know who you are because he told me 'what a fucking player he is'. He told me that if you were playing in South America, you'd be a superstar, but that you're not suited to English football."

Terry Venables used to tell me that if I'd been born in Brazil, I'd be in the World XI and today, I honestly believe I'd be a top Premier League player because of how the game has changed.

I had unbelievable skill, technique, and speed – but what I couldn't do was tackle, head the ball – I was useless! Back then, they wanted to chase back, tackle, compete in the air and get kicked to fucking pieces. That's just how it was back then. I guess I just played in the wrong era.

Meanwhile, back at the Orient and back to the real world as it was then. I was aged 30 now, and still had a few years left in me and I remembered Terry Venables once telling me that I would one day make a great manager. He said, "Silks, just stick to what you know, and you'll be brilliant." The problem was, I was a coach and I believe I was world class only at one thing – making players better on an individual basis.

I would take one or two players at a time, and I would make them 30-40% better after just one season. I'd done it for TV at Palace, again on a player-by-player basis. But as for coaching a whole squad, I didn't have a clue and was way out of my comfort zone.

When Frank had given me the job, he had watched me work with players one-on-one and he said, "I've never seen anyone do what you do."

But he hadn't realised I had shortcomings elsewhere!

At my first training session as a coach, Frank said to me, "Can you take the back four, Silks?"

I said, "Take them where?"

He said, "I don't care, just take them."

So I said, "Okay, Ladbrokes or a café?"

He asked me what I was talking about. I said, "Frank, I can't coach."

He told me I could, and he'd seen me doing it, but I said what he'd seen was me working on an individual basis, not as a group.

THE ORIENT EXPRESS

He asked if I was joking or not. Then he asked me to take the back four to go through a drill where they pushed up as a unit and I said, "Frank, I haven't got a fucking clue."

He asked again if I was pulling his leg, but then realised I wasn't. "I've made you a player-coach and you can't fucking coach?"

I said, "Well, when you gave me the job, you never asked if I could do it. You offered me the job and I took it. My forte is judgement of players and individual coaching. Front three? Midfield four? Back four? Whatever it is, I am fucking useless. I can't do it and don't understand it."

I was effectively Frank's No.2 by default!

I was playing regularly, coaching players to my strengths and working on the odd set-piece routine and that's how it went. When Frank would finish his pre-match talk, he'd always say, "Silks, do you want to add anything?" And if I'd seen something or thought something might work, I'd chip in with a few words. I nicked a few ideas from Terry Venables and then added my own touch to it and a lot of them were very effective. One involved a free-kick outside the box – maybe five yards or so and slightly to the side of the D.

The idea was that if the opposition put five men in the wall and maybe one 'draught excluder' on the floor – and they will also have one loose in the wall in case the ball is rolled to the side for a shot. That's seven players and the keeper accounted for. That leaves three players to defend. Have one of your players on the ball and one to the left, so another of the opposition needs to cover the possibility of playing it in behind the wall from an angle. Two players are left to mark the far post where your player will cross the ball and if you overload that back post – staggering your players around the box to begin with – good luck defending that ball in.

It was something TV had done, and it worked at Orient four out of five times and numerous other times at my other clubs. Nobody ever does that in today's game, yet it's so simple and effective! It's almost impossible to defend against.

I did it in training with Martin Allen once and it was successful eight times out of ten – he said he'd never seen anything like it.

But our lack of finances was stopping us progressing. It was killing us, in fact.

The 1982/83 season wasn't much better than the year before in terms of results and we ended up just avoiding a second successive relegation, but it could have been so different. Before the season began, I'd been watching France at the 1982 World Cup and I said to Frank, "Let's play five at the back."

He asked what I meant, and I said, "We're gonna have three centre-backs. Didn't you see how France were playing?" He said he hadn't but he was interested. "They played with three central defenders with their full-backs pushed up on the wings – that's how we're gonna play and I'll explain why. Our best players are also our three defenders: Tommy Cunningham, Colin Foster and Pat Corbett. Our two full-backs are David Stride and Kevin Hales – who do you think out of those two is the best defender?"

Frank said neither, but they were both good going forward. My reasoning was that if we had a back four, we'd have to leave out one of our best defenders and have two full-backs who were better attacking, so we're weakening our defence. A back five gets the best out of everyone and Frank smiled and said, "Fuck me, Silks. Let's do that in training and see how it goes."

We trained to that blueprint, and I thought we were magnificent. The lads got it straight away, went with it and our pre-season was stunning.

We had a pre-season friendly against Wimbledon and we murdered them 5-0. They couldn't live with us, or figure out what we were doing differently. After the game, the Wimbledon owner, Sam Hammam, said to Frank, "I don't know how you did that, but your lads are the best I've ever seen at this level." He then told us he was sticking £5,000 on us to win Division Three at 25-1!

Everything seemed to be coming together and in the

first game of the '82/83 season we were away to Chesterfield and it's no exaggeration to say that if we'd taken all our first-half chances, we'd have gone in 15-0 up! We were that dominant and created chance after chance. But we'd only scored one and in the second half, Pat Corbett got caught with a late challenge and Pat being Pat, he got up and knocked the guy out and was sent off.

That was the start of everything going wrong. He was suspended for five or six games and when he came back, Tommy Cunningham was injured – when he came back, Colin Foster did his hamstring… we never had all three players available together at the same time again that season, had to play a back four again and ended up back to where we'd started, just avoiding the drop. It was unbelievable and I'm still convinced to this day that if we'd had players who could have come in, we'd have won that league by a country mile, but we only had a squad of 16 and didn't even have kids to bring in.

As an example to file under the 'what might have been' section, the following illustrates the sort of financial restrictions we were operating under.

During a pre-season friendly against Gillingham, I identified a central defender and a striker that I knew would be fantastic for us and told Frank. He told me to get the job done and if they were open to the move, to then speak with the chairman. I spoke to both lads after the game and they both said they'd be happy to join Orient. I went to the owner, Neville Ovenden.

I told him we had to sign both players and that Gillingham wanted £30,000 for each player. I told him they would make a massive difference to our team, and said I thought I could negotiate them down to £40,000 for the pair, but he said, "No, I've only got £30,000 – just buy one of them."

I met with Frank, and he asked which one we should buy? I told him that normally I'd say to get the striker, because we didn't have many goals in our team, but on the other hand, we couldn't keep them out at the other end, so I honestly didn't know. We needed both.

Frank told me to go back to Gillingham and negotiate. So I did.

I went along, met the owner again, and after a lot of talk and convincing, we did a deal for the pair for £35,000 – plus a 20% sell-on clause if we ever sold them, something that nobody had ever done at that time. I'd got the idea from a place in Whitechapel Market that was selling items that if you bought two, you got 20% off. I thought, why not just add 20% on to our deal for the Gillingham lads?

I went back to our chairman and told him about this fantastic deal I'd agree for the club, and he said, "No. I've not got the extra money. It's not happening."

So we signed neither. The defender's name was

Steve Bruce, and the striker was Tony Cascarino, and we could have had them both for peanuts and made a fortune on them within a couple of years.

I think it's safe to say they went on to have pretty good careers, but as disappointed as I was, the whole process of finding talent, negotiating, and coming up with innovative ways of making a deal happen had lit a flame inside me because I'd loved it. I didn't know it at the time, but I was already laying the foundations for the end of my playing career.

Chapter 11

DISORIENTATED!

Frank Clark did extremely well at Orient given what he had to work with player-wise and financially, and I don't think Brian Clough could have done better with the resources we had at that time.

We paid one of the lowest average wages in the league, and being a London club, that's where 90% of our player recruitment came from. With so many clubs around or near us, most of our signings were, for the want of a better word, cast-offs from bigger teams in the capital – basically players other London clubs didn't want.

Pat Corbett had been at Tottenham, Tommy Cunningham had been at QPR, John Cornwall came from the youth team, David Stride came from Southampton,

Kevin Godfrey, Shaun Brooks, and Mark McNeil were all Londoners – so more or less every member of the squad was either a Londoner or from not that far away. We just didn't have the money to entice players from further afield and many of our lads were still living at home because they couldn't afford to move out.

None of it was ideal and the three years I was there in a coaching capacity were very difficult, and the results on the pitch weren't much better. We had a fantastic group of lads and a good team spirit, but aside from our keepers, our squad amounted to 14 senior players.

We couldn't rotate the team, there was no competition for places and if we had injuries, we'd have to bring in 16 and 17-year-olds with little or no experience from our youth team. We had no other choice, and the coaching staff would need to join in the training games just to make up the numbers. It was madness.

After the third year, my time at the club had come to a natural end. I went to see Frank and we both agreed the time was right for me to move on.

It was completely cordial and was something I'd been thinking about for some time. Frank wanted to take the club forward, but try as I might, I couldn't help him progress it, so we called time on our working relationship and I left the club.

It was 1985 and, meanwhile, Terry Venables' career

was going in a completely different direction as I learned he'd not long been appointed manager of Barcelona!

He called me out of the blue one day and I was always happy to hear his voice. I said, "Please tell me you are calling to ask if I want to sign for Barcelona and play alongside Diego Maradona?"

He just laughed and said, "Not this time, Silks, sorry!"

I said, "Fantastic. I'm your first signing at Crystal Palace, your first signing at QPR and now you're at Barcelona and you don't fucking want me?"

If nothing else he'd given me a great line for any after dinner speaking I did in the future!

Our disagreement at QPR had been long forgotten and he just laughed and said that, sadly, it was just a chat on this occasion. Imagine that, though? Barry Silkman signs for Barcelona? I tried, believe me.

The actual reason he called me up, as he had done throughout his managerial career, was to ask me advice on players, which I'd always considered to be a huge compliment. Even more so now he was managing one of the biggest clubs in the world. Whenever I gave my opinion, he always seemed to take it without question.

He said, "Silks, I've got a big problem and he goes by the name of Diego Maradona. He's lost a yard – if not two yards – of pace and every single thing goes through him. When any of the players get the ball, they just want to give it to him and I want to play fast, quick attacking football. I want to go forwards and play with a style that hurts the opposition, not go backwards or sideways and he's slowing everything down. I've got this German guy called Bernd Schuster and I want him to dictate play because if he does, I think we'll go on and win La Liga. If not, I've got a big problem. I need to go to the president and tell him I think we need to move Maradona on, but I don't think he will sanction it."

I said, "TV, you've got one period when you are strongest as a manager, and that's when you first go in."

He said, "But what if I win the league?"

I said, "If you win the league with a club like Barcelona, everybody will want your job and if you don't win it in the second year, you'll be thought of as a failure. So the only time you're in a position of strength is when you first walk into a club, so now is the time. You have to tell the president you don't want him."

TV could see what I was saying and said, "You're bang on, Silks. I'll do it. I'm going to tell him I don't want him in my team."

And he did.

A few weeks later, he called me back and said, "Silks, I've had absolute murders with the president, but I've won. Maradona's out. Now I have to make this team at least five points better than last season, because if I can't make them better than they were with Maradona in the side, I'll pack in football."

DISORIENTATED!

It took a lot of guts, but he'd won the day and Barcelona did go on to win La Liga for the first time in 11 years. TV invited me over to Catalonia to join the celebrations at the end of that season, but I couldn't make it at the time for one reason or another. Though I'd never met Diego Maradona – and I'm fairly sure he'd never heard of me – it's funny that I played a small part (or maybe a much bigger role) in the future of the best player on the planet at the time. Of course, he went to Napoli, which turned out to be the perfect club for him, but I guess he never knew that a Third Division midfielder in England had helped decide his departure from the Nou Camp! That said, for all I know he could have engineered my move from QPR!

Back in the real world – and literally later the same day I'd left Orient – I got a call from Bobby Moore, who was then manager at Southend United. I'd known Bobby since I'd been a schoolboy at West Ham and kept in touch over the years, and he told me the reason he was calling was he wanted me to go and play for him.

I was 33, hadn't had any thoughts about hanging my boots up just yet, and you don't say no to Bobby Moore. I was thinking 'what was the worst that could happen?' and so I went along to see for myself.

Harry Cripps was the coach at the time, and I soon discovered there was a great atmosphere at the club. It was Bobby's second season at Roots Hall, having guided the team narrowly away from re-election in his first year.

The wages were nothing to write home about, but I thought it might be a nice swansong to my playing career. I knew the town of Southend really well, had always liked it, so I agreed a short-term deal with the chairman and signed for Bobby.

My first real contribution was to tell Bobby to sign Richard Cadette from Orient as his contract was expiring – I don't think Frank was too pleased with that – but he wanted to come and play with me and my loyalties were with my new club now. Though I think they paid about £4,000 for him, it would turn out to be one of the best pieces of business Southend United ever did.

Ironically, Cadette scored four goals on his debut – against Orient would you believe! He would bang in 56 goals in 104 appearances at Roots Hall before they made something like 25 times the amount they'd paid a couple of years later when he left for Sheffield United.

The financial restraints at Southend were similar to Orient but the lads were fantastic, and I really enjoyed my time there.

Bobby was one of the nicest men I'd ever met in football, but it was my honest opinion that he just wasn't cut out for management. He didn't have the heart to drop players, he didn't have the heart to tell a player they weren't good enough – he just didn't have that inside him, because he was too empathetic with people. The sad fact is that you have to have that nasty side when needed to succeed as a manager.

It didn't mean I liked him any less – and probably made me like him more. He was just a decent human being who didn't want to hurt anyone. It was never going to work out for him, though. Football is littered with great players who weren't great managers.

At one of his first team meetings, one of my new team-mates, Alan Rogers, had tipped me off about something Bobby would say time and time again. He'd told me he used a word that didn't actually exist and to see if I could spot what it was.

So, at the first team talk I was listening intently when Bobby said it – and that word was 'irregardless'. I looked over at Alan and we both almost burst out laughing. Bobby the man – I loved him; but Bobby the manager, unfortunately, struggled and was a polar opposite to Bobby Moore the footballer.

The training sessions were similar to Orient in that we barely had any players – it was madness – so Bobby would join in, and we had a game – First Team v Reserves. At the end I went over to Bobby and said, "You need to be playing, Bob – you're the best centre-half we've got at the club." And he was.

He was 44 at the time but his timing was still unbelievable, and he was still in fantastic shape, but he just said, "Silks, I can't – I'm too old". But he was still so good, so fit and his metabolism meant he hadn't put an ounce on since he stopped playing. But after the career he'd had, he didn't want to put his boots on again and play other than in training matches when he pretty much had to.

He loved a drink did Bob, and occasionally that spilled into his working life.

On one occasion, we had an evening game at home, and it got to 7.20pm and we still hadn't seen any sign of Bob. Harry Cripps had shared the team with us, with the size of the squad meaning it pretty much picked itself, and as we were getting changed, in came Bobby – with, of all people, Malcolm Allison in tow.

To say they were a little bit worse for wear due to the drink was an understatement and we were about 25 minutes away from kick-off with a manager who was paralytic! The lads were chuckling as Bob gave his team-talk which was slightly slurred as he said, "Boys, you all know what you've got to do." And that was that! He walked out again.

I was at a stage of my life when my one desire was to get back into music, but I couldn't figure out a way to do it. I was still helping people out, doing backing vocals and in and around the music world on a regular basis. When most of the lads were thinking about how to deal with the threat Grimsby Town posed, I was sat there thinking, 'Could I still be a singing star aged 34?' I wasn't interested in anything else.

The owner of Brentford had approached me several times. He was involved in acting and he sent me a letter while I was at Southend asking if I was interested in a couple of parts in films he was involved with. He thought I'd be perfect for what he had in mind and told me to get out of football because he'd make me a millionaire through acting. But for whatever reason, it didn't appeal to me. All I wanted to do was get on stage, have a bit of banter with the punters and sing some songs, so I never took him up on it.

After the game where Bobby had been drunk – we got beat, by the way – he left the club, leaving us managerless. The owner, Vic Jobson, asked to see one of our senior players at the time, Paul Clark, and asked him if he'd take over as manager, but he said he wanted me to work alongside him as he thought I was the most knowledgeable football man he'd ever worked with. The owner was fine with that, so Clarky asked me if I would be his No.2 at Southend United, pick the team and focus on skills while he'd be the hard man of the partnership. It would be a classic good cop, bad cop situation that would remain in place until the end of the season when Clarky's position would be reviewed.

I thought, 'why not?' and we had about a dozen games to the end of the campaign, and I think we won seven and lost five, drawing none. I brought a couple of players in who Bobby hadn't been using and went with three central defenders, something I'd wanted to do at Orient before injuries scuppered the plan.

We had three really good centre-backs, but Danny O'Shea wasn't really a full-back – more a wide midfielder – and our other full-back was Glenn Pennyfather, who went on to have a great career with Ipswich Town but was more of an attacker than a defender and he was definitely more effective in the attacking third of the pitch.

So, we lined up with three central defenders – one, Stevie Hatter, was so slow that I had to think carefully about his role. I told him not to drop off, he had to keep right up the arse of the opposition No.9 and then told another, Shane Westley, he was Stevie's cover because he was like greased lightning. I said, "Anything goes behind Steve, I want you to mop up." Our third defender was also quick and I put him on the right of the three.

We were outstanding in a lot of those games and our form in the weeks that remained was really good – we were never in with a chance of going up, but we finished in a healthy ninth in the Third Division. Clarky generously told Vic Jobson our improvement had all been down to me because of the way I'd set the team up and Vic called me in to his office and I sat down facing him over his desk.

"Right," he said. "I want to make you player-coach next season, Silky, and I want you to oversee the coaching throughout the entire club as well."

Here we go again, I thought...

I wasn't a coach, as I'd stated many times before, but because a lot of the senior pros were low maintenance, I thought it might be possible. I'd sort of done the same at Orient, so it wasn't entirely unchartered territory, but I could see a problem. Clarky's role was unlikely to be permanent and the fact was he'd been told he was only keeping the seat warm for somebody else. When a new manager was employed, he would have to step aside, so I said to Vic, "That's all fine, but what happens when the new guy comes in? He'll want to do things his way. He won't want to inherit a coach."

Vic said, "Silks, don't worry – the new manager will know you are the coach. You'll be in charge of the first team, reserve and youth teams and focus on the football side of the club, and I want you to get all the coaches in and set everything up the way you want it."

He prepared a contract for me, which I collected and put in my inside jacket pocket in an envelope, but I hadn't signed it as yet. I was still very wary that a new guy might not want me to be involved. That night, I went to watch a Crystal Palace reserve game and before the match, I went in to see Palace chairman Ron

Noades to see if I could ask his advice on something. He said, "Silks, of course, no problem, come into my office at half-time."

So, I went in and explained to Ron I'd been offered the job of chief coach at Southend where I'd be in charge of the first team, reserves, and youth side. I took out the contract Vic had prepared for me and showed it to Ron, explaining that as I would only be actively coaching the first team, it was a player-coach contract in effect. He looked at it and said, "Silks, this is brilliant. It's exactly what you wanted. What's the problem?"

I asked Ron what he thought would happen if the new manager didn't want me as his first-team coach. He said, "Well, he'll have to accept it. You're in charge and he'll have to go along with it or else he shouldn't take the job."

Then I asked Ron what he'd do if he was me. He said, "Silks, are you crazy? Sign it and take it back to Vic and say thank you very much." So I did. I signed it and handed it back to Vic the next day and that was that – I was now a sort of coaching overlord at Southend United, as well as being a contracted player-coach. The season was now over, so I made plans for a break before I started thinking about pre-season and what we'd be doing for the new campaign.

Shortly before pre-season, it was announced that

DISORIENTATED!

David Webb had been given the job as new manager of Southend United.

For me, that was the worst appointment they could have made because Webb's knowledge of football was between zero and minus 10 – and that wasn't my assumption; he'd told me so himself!

He was part-owner of a car dealership in Camden Town with a good friend of mine, Lawrence Metz, and my relationship with Webb was mainly knowing him as a player and obviously occasionally seeing him at the dealership.

Around seven years prior to me taking the Southend coaching role – I think I was playing for Palace at the time – I'd gone to see Lawrence to discuss possibly getting a new car and Webby turned up. We exchanged greetings and he said to Lawrence, "I can't believe it – I've just become manager of Bournemouth." Lawrence congratulated him and I said, "Well done, Webby."

He replied, "Yeah, well sort of well done. The problem I've got is I know fuck all about coaching, I know fuck all about picking a team and know fuck all about whether a player is any good or not."

That stuck in my mind for obvious reasons and though he initially did okay at Bournemouth, he fell out with the chairman, was moved on and then got a job at Torquay United, where it was a bit of a disaster, and they finished bottom of the Fourth Division twice in succession.

Webby knew Vic Jobson well as they had done business together and obviously kept in touch, and Vic had offered him the job, which he accepted. That sort of thing happens more often than you'd think in football, with the old maxim 'it's not necessarily what you know, more who you know'. Once I heard the news, I went to see Vic and said, "Look, David Webb is not going to want me at this club."

Vic said, "No Silky, he's not said anything like that at all."

I said, "Trust me – he will not want me at this club."

I left it at that and then arrived on the first day of pre-season training and from the minute we started training, he made it very clear that I was going to be a problem for him.

We had a running session one day and Webby had no idea that I was a fantastic runner in all disciplines – sprints or long distance. When I was 15, I'd won at the Southern England Championships in the 100 metres, 200 metres, 800 metres and the cross country and I could run all day. Anyone who had ever played with me knew that I was a natural athlete and on this one particular day, I was about to piss Webby off.

The session was called 'increase and demand' and was centred around three football pitches. You had

Fresh-faced and happy as a player at Manchester City in the late 1970s

Mum and Dad, Jinny and Sam, didn't have much but gave me everything I needed

Mum – pictured with me and my daughter, Keenia – was a strong lady

Working hard as a Crystal Palace player in 1977, though I was better known for my skills and tricks

At Leyton Orient I took my first steps into coaching

On the bench in my City days with Malcolm Allison – who was quite the character, putting it mildly – and Tony Book

I enjoyed my time at QPR with a great bunch of lads and a manager, in Terry Venables, who trusted me. Here I am *(left)* after scoring against West Ham in 1980

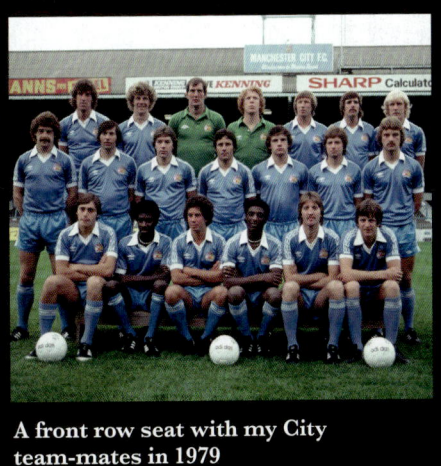

A front row seat with my City team-mates in 1979

Trying to find a way through against my former club, Crystal Palace, at Maine Road in 1979

There were fantastic times socialising with football legend George Best and comedy genius Billy Connolly. This picture was taken in 1979

With great friend Terry Venables, Don Shanks and Stan Bowles, all once of QPR

I even met 'The Greatest', Muhammad Ali, in his later years

A recent meeting with former football club owner Michael Knighton

A night at Bootleggers in the 1980s with Bill Wyman

Picture by Hyacinth Money

Top: The talented Tony Currie
Top right: With Barry Fry and David Sullivan while holding my grandson Eran
Right: I managed Mike Tyson in the UK
Above: The character that is Ian Holloway

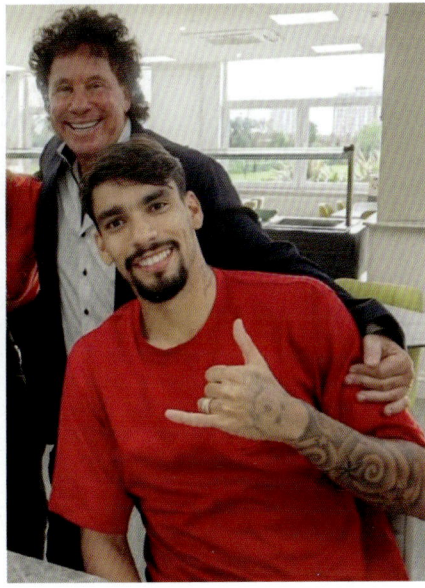

I've had many deadlings with renowned agent Pini Zahavi *(left)* over the years, and I helped to bring Brazilian star Lucas Paqueta from France to West Ham in 2022

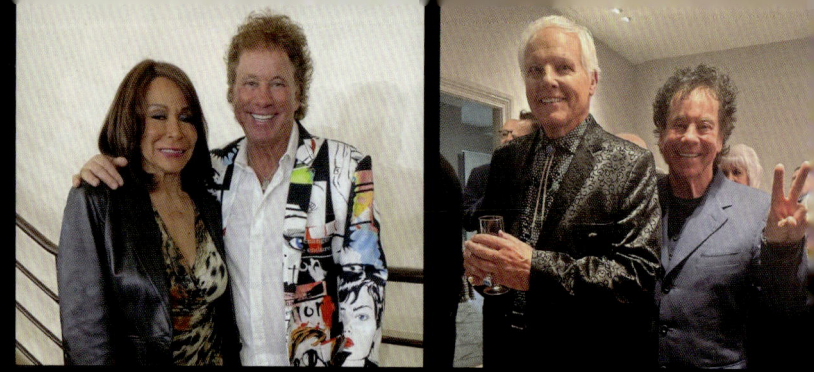

I cherish friendships with lots of stars including *(l-r)* Freda Payne, Jess Conrad

I've been really close to Billy Ocean through the years, though I know him better as Les Charles. Also pictured are Chico and Debbie Sledge

Des O'Connor (pictured with my daughter Keenia) and Bradley Walsh

Keenia with Tito Jackson

A recent picture with Kid Creole and Jeffrey Daniel

I helped Alexander O'Neal get his career back on track. Here we are with his wife Cynthia, Keenia and Eran

One of my favourite groups, Tavares, with Keenia in 1998, and with me in 2023

Ally and I shared special times, including a trip to Kenya in 1995 *(left)*, the place that inspired our daughter's name Keenia *(right)*. Ally and daughter Danielle *(middle)*

My son, Saul, and his mother, Rachel

I've tried to keep myself fit over the years. Here I am taking part in a legends tournament in 2014

Footballer, entertainer, greyhound trainer, agent – it's been a rich and varied career...so far

DISORIENTATED!

to do various length runs that increased in distance and intensity each time and I'd finished in front each time. The last run was the longest – about a four-minute circuit – and I hit the front again alongside Shane Westley. Webby shouted over, "Fucking beat him, Shane, fucking beat him!" I shouted over, "Webby, I haven't even got out of first gear, yet."

I said to Shane to pick it up and he said, "Silks, I'm flat out." So I said I couldn't hang around any longer and pulled about 25 yards clear, and as I passed Webby, I said, "Do you want to put somebody in now?" As I finished, I looked at him and he had a face like thunder. So I kept running and did the entire circuit again and when I finished, all the lads were clapping me.

Webby said, "Right, I want you in at seven this evening to work with Buster Footman."

Buster was the physio, so I went in as requested and Buster said, "Silks, I don't even know what to do – there's nothing I can suggest that you don't find easy, so go home and I'll just tell the manager we did a load of terrace work."

After that, Webby told me to train on my own and immediately, by doing that, he was putting the club in breach of contract and technically, I was now available as a free transfer.

So, I trained on my own and took part in the bigger sessions.

The next day, at training, we had an 11-a-side game with me playing for the reserves against the first team and we got a corner. On the sidelines, Webby was busy telling everyone where he wanted them at the corner and while they were chattering and organising, I called for a short corner, the lad from the youth team played it to me on the corner of the box, and I looked up and curled it over the keeper and into the roof of the net.

Webby exploded. "Who told you to take a fucking short corner?"

I said, "What? What do you think is going to happen against the team you're playing on Friday night? Do you think they're going to ask your advice on what sort of corner they can take? Are you fucking mad?"

He had a face like thunder and said, "Go back to the ground." I shrugged my shoulders and said that was no problem. He added he wanted me in at 9pm that evening to work with Buster. I got changed and went back to the ground that evening only to find it all locked up! That was the final straw and if Webb wanted to take me on, no problem.

The next day, I went in and handed in 14 days' notice for breach of contract and said I would be staying at home for those 14 days. The club strongly objected to my stance and within a week, we were at a tribunal, and by a minor miracle, the chairman of the tribunal was… Ron Noades! Ron already knew about the contract

DISORIENTATED!

I'd signed because I had asked his advice a few weeks earlier. Brendon Batson was my PFA representative, and I said, "Brendon, do me a favour – apart from stating my name, don't say a word."

He asked what I meant. I said, "You know I'm nailed on to win this, and I'm winning this like you wouldn't believe. Let them dig themselves a hole."

The tribunal began, with Vic Jobson making a statement and then David Webb stepped up, but I couldn't believe what he was coming out with. As a player, he'd had a very good career but, in my opinion, he wasn't cut out to be a manager and I found him not to be the nicest person. As he continued to dig a deeper and deeper hole with the things he was coming out with, I just sat there listening to it all utterly bemused, and stopped short of laughing on one or two occasions.

It got to a stage where Noades had heard enough. He said to Vic Jobson, "Vic, why did you give Barry the contract in the first place?"

Vic said, "Because he blackmailed me."

Ron said, "How did he blackmail you exactly?"

Vic responded, "Well, he said he'd leave the club if I didn't give him the contract he wanted and if he left, a load of other players would leave too because they were only there because of him."

Ron looked at him and said, "Vic, I'm going to stop this now and stop you embarrassing yourself any further." He then asked us all to leave the room while the panel deliberated.

We must have been out about five minutes when we were invited back in. Ron said, "Okay, this is situation. You're going to pay Barry half of the contract you agreed within seven days, and the remainder before the 25th of December."

Vic protested, "But we haven't done anything wrong."

Ron said, "Vic, I know all about the contract because Barry came to me for advice as to whether he should sign it or not because he was so concerned that the new manager wouldn't want him – so both of you have gone down in my estimation. Luckily, I stopped you very early on."

In spite of everything, I was disappointed with the way it had ended with Vic.

I'd got the result I wanted, went home, and wondered whether I should finally pack the game in now or not. I had some serious thinking to do, and I had a Saturday morning lie-in the next day for the first time in a while.

Then, at around 10am, my phone rang – it was Dario Gradi.

I'd worked with Dario a couple of years before when he was a youth team coach at Crystal Palace, and he had quickly formed an impression of me as some sort of arrogant wide boy. As it was, he admitted he'd got it wrong and told me he'd actually loved working with me and the moment my playing career ended, he would ask me to be his assistant manager. And here we were.

He said, "Right, I hear you've left Southend, so why don't you come up and be my assistant?"

I laughed and said, "Okay Dario, where are you?"

He said, "Crewe."

When I asked where that was he repeated, "Crewe, in Cheshire."

I said, "Dario, are you mad? I'm not coming all the way up there!"

But he was insistent. "Look, you'll love it. Come up, have a look around and see what you think."

So I did. Crewe wasn't much to write home about, but Dario was building something, and he had a youth set-up as good as any I'd come across in my career.

Dario took me to one side after showing me around and said, "Silks, give it a go. Just sign a contract until the end of the season, see if you like it and see if you enjoy your football. If you do, stay for two or three years."

Dario knew I could spot a player, so I accepted the offer and joined Crewe Alexandra in 1986.

I moved north for the second time in my career and started life at Gresty Road.

Dario's first task for me was to go and watch a Manchester United reserve game.

He said, "Silks, we've got a player we're looking at

and I'm not sure if I want to sign him or not. I've had different reports from people at the club – some saying yes, some saying no – but I trust your judgement and want you to see him."

Dario and I went along, and the game was only 10 minutes old, and this player had touched the ball once with his toe.

I said to Dario, "We've got to sign him."

He laughed and said, "He's not even touched the ball yet!"

I said, "I know, but he's already made so many unbelievable runs into space and the reason he's not touched it is that either nobody has seen his runs, they don't have the ability to find him, or they don't want to pass it."

Dario said, "Yeah but if he'd been put clear five times, he might have missed all five."

"True," I said, "but he might have scored all five as well. If he'd scored even one you'd already be wanting to sign him – I'm telling you, he will get at least a goal every other game. You've got to sign him."

Dario smiled, nodded and said this lad's mum and dad were at the game and he'd see if he could get a deal done. And he did.

We signed him, and I didn't think much more about it because I was only at Crewe a few weeks. My girlfriend Mandy didn't want to leave her job in London, and I was at a stage where I didn't really want to be conducting a long distance relationship, so I told Dario I was heading back to London, purely on the basis that it wasn't working out on a personal level.

He understood completely and said he still wanted me to keep an eye out for players he could sign if and when I came across them, and I told him that was no problem.

Fast forwarding slightly, three years later Dario called me.

He said, "You know that player you convinced me to sign? We've been offered £150,000 but I think we can get more."

I said it sounded like good business, but he insisted he was going to hold out for more – and he did. He got £200,000 from Aston Villa and the player in question was future England skipper David Platt.

I didn't have much time at Crewe, but I'd like to think I played a small part in making sure the club stayed profitable for a year or two!

As for my career, there were no clubs queuing up to sign me and I was at a loose end. I was only 34 years old and fit as a fiddle but I couldn't see myself playing on and I didn't really want to be a coach. There was always the possibility of utilising my eye for a promising player somehow, but as it was, I was a bit jaded with football and as the weeks and months passed by, I sort of fell out of love with the game. I still wanted to fulfil my dreams as a singer, so there were possibilities, but at that particular time I wasn't exactly sure where my future lay.

Ask any former player and they will tell you when that day comes, it's one of the saddest days of your life.

Chapter 12

THE 'WHAT MIGHT HAVE BEEN' CHAPTER

One of my biggest regrets in life is not making it as a singer, because if I had got the breaks I needed and been able to embark on a recording career, I would have jacked football in without hesitation because singing was my true passion.

And in my mid-20s, that could – and should – have happened.

At the time I was regularly turning out for Jess Conrad's Showbiz XI with people like 'Diddy' David

Hamilton, Bill Kenwright, Billy Idol and Chris Quinten, and thousands would turn up to take pictures and get autographs from their heroes.

I'd not long recorded a demo for Barry Mason, writer of 'Delilah' who was looking to place a song he'd written for a boy and girl group.

The song was called 'As Long As I Have You' and it was never going to be for me, but he wanted to hear what it sounded like in a studio.

I was the only professional footballer involved in the Showbiz XI, and after one game, I got speaking to this guy who had been playing on our team called Dave – that was as much as I knew about him.

I was in the shower singing the song Barry Mason had got me to sing and when I came out, Dave says to me, "Fuck me, you can sing a bit. Have you ever been in a studio or is that a stupid question?"

I told him I'd been in studios on well over 100 occasions, that I'd had an agent when I was 16, but I'd left that all behind and never really pursued a singing career after that.

Dave said, "Next week, my brother is playing for the Showbiz XI. I'd like you to pick him up and take him to the game and play one of your demos to him." He then asked if I had anything he could listen to, so I took him to my car and played the 'As Long As I Have You' demo that I'd duetted with a female session singer.

THE 'WHAT MIGHT HAVE BEEN' CHAPTER

He smiled and said, "Fuck me, you can really sing. You've got to play that to my brother. You're really good."

I didn't have a clue who Dave's brother was, and I assumed he would have forgotten about it in a few days – just bluster that people do from time to time. He gave me the address of his brother – El Rancho in Totteridge – and asked if I'd pick him up the following Sunday and take him to the game.

So, I did.

I arrived at this very beautiful property, and out walks Mickie Most – the famous music producer I mentioned earlier – with a woman I presumed to be his wife. Of course, Mickie was huge at the time and was a powerful man in the record industry. I thought there was no way I was playing my demo to Mickie Most. No chance!

He got in and introduced himself and his wife Christina and I said I knew who he was, and it was good to meet him.

Halfway along the journey, Mickie says, "Dave says you have something to play for me?"

I was cringing inside but, in the end, just thought, "Fuck it. Why not?" and put the tape in.

When the song ended, Mickie said, "I don't like the song or the female singer, but I love the guy's voice."

I just said, "Oh, okay." And left it like that. We played the game later and afterwards, I dropped him home and he said it had been lovely to meet me and I said likewise. Then we went our separate ways.

It was during the close season, so I didn't have any games to play or training and a few days later, the phone rings and a woman asks if she could speak to Barry Silkman. I said, "Speaking…" She told me Mickie Most wanted to speak with me, and then he came on the phone and said, "Silk – you little fucker. You didn't tell me that was you singing on that demo! Would you like to come down to my studio later this week?"

That was the start of it.

I became a vocalist, backing singer and sang demos for Mickie Most, the UK's most influential music producer. I would work a lot with Hot Chocolate and Errol Brown and loads of other household names, doing what I loved whenever Mickie needed me to do something. It didn't affect my playing career and as long as I was singing, I was a happy bunny.

That would go on for around 18 months. One time, Mickie and Christina invited me and Mandy out on a Friday evening, but I had to decline as I had a game the next day. He told me it was an early dinner and that it would be worth my while to attend, so I decided to go along.

It was a nice restaurant in London, and we were chatting away when Christina asked, "Do you really want to sing or just be friends with Mickie?"

THE 'WHAT MIGHT HAVE BEEN' CHAPTER

I told her I wanted to be a singer and if it happened, it happened and if it didn't, I was happy continuing to be a footballer. I said, "Christina, I'm not sure I understand the question."

Mickie then said, "We've found a song for you. And I think you'd be the ideal person to sing it. We've found a couple actually, both are good, but one is amazing."

Christina then said, "We are going to turn you into the biggest music artist this country has ever seen. Forget Tom Jones, you are going to be mega."

I said, "Chris, from your mouth to God's ears."

Mickie asked me to come along to the studio on Monday and collect the tapes and give the songs a listen, then let him know what I thought.

I was living with Mandy at the time, and when I got home, I told her I couldn't believe what was happening.

I couldn't wait to hear the songs and I collected them on the Monday and listened to the first one called 'Clown', which was okay but didn't rock my world exactly. The second song, however, I absolutely fucking loved.

It was a ballad and after four or five listens, I knew every word and exactly how I wanted to sing it, so I called Mickie and told him what I thought and that I loved one of the tracks.

He said, "Yeah, I know which one – the ballad. The only problem is, Silk, if you have a ballad as your first hit, it's very difficult to follow up with a pop song but come along tomorrow and let's record it."

I went along, we did two takes and he said, "You've nailed it – you've sang it unbelievably well and we've got what we need."

I was absolutely buzzing. It was really happening, and I couldn't have been happier.

Mickie did a rough mix and he told me I'd need to pop along for the final mix and then we were done.

The following Sunday, I went along to play poker at Mickie's house along with Errol Brown and his wife Jeanette and the guy who owned French Connection called Stephen Marks – as well as Mickie and Christina. They were all fucking multi-millionaires, and I barely had a pot to piss in!

It was a nightmare because they were winning hands of £500 or £600, but I just about survived.

A week later, the game was being held at another house and so I swung by to pick Mickie and Chris up, but Mickie said he couldn't make it this time and to just take Chris with me. She sat in the front, and I drove, but she started putting her hand on my leg, so I shifted away. I wasn't having any of it. We were at a guy called Lenny's house – he was a successful estate agent and as I drove along the driveway, Errol and Jeanette were looking out. As we left my car, Chris took hold of my arm, and I didn't know what to say. We must have

THE 'WHAT MIGHT HAVE BEEN' CHAPTER

looked like a married couple, and I was really uncomfortable. I said, "Anyone would think we were married," for a laugh and she said, "Well, you never know, Silk."

Uh-oh…

We started playing cards and Chris, who was a huge wine drinker, was soon worse for wear. She was secretly instructing me what to play and how, until it was just me and her – but she didn't have a hand and eventually just said, "I'm not going to see you this time – I can't win. You win."

I'd won a big pile of cash – as much as I'd ever had – and then I took her back to Montebello and she kept putting her hand on my leg and I was thinking, 'how the hell do I get out of this?'

We arrived back at one in the morning, and she asked me to come in as it was important. I said, "It's way too late for me, Chris – I need to get off." But she insisted, so I walked into the house and Mickie was still up watching TV. Chris saw he was awake and just said, "Fuck it."

Mickie had got up and was coming into the hallway and said, "What did she just say?" I said, I didn't know as I wasn't listening but I needed to get home.

The next day, I was asked to take the cassette back of the song I recorded and afterwards I tried calling Mickie, maybe 10 times, but he never picked up.

It would be 14 years before I heard from him again

and I remember my mobile going off and I recognised the number straight away. It was Mickie. I said, "Hello?"

"Silks, you won't know who this is…"

I said, "I do, Mickie, because I've never forgotten your number. And I recognise your voice."

He asked me to do him a huge favour and meet him in Regents Park, which I agreed to do. We ended up walking around the park about three times and he explained that Christina's way out of the situation the following day was to say I'd got hold of her. But six months later, she'd told him during a drunken argument that she'd made the whole thing up and that I hadn't actually done anything.

"I was too embarrassed to call you," he said.

It had taken him 14 years to tell me and by that time, I'd lost my edge and the stomach to really pursue a music career. I still did bits and pieces and had plenty of offers, but in my eyes, that had been my chance and it had been taken away from me through no fault of my own… it just wasn't meant to be.

Some years later, I was at David Sullivan's house, and he'd hired Rick Astley for a party, and he was singing when he started handing the mic around. When he came to me, my wife at the time said, "Wrong person." But I sang anyway, and then Rick went and sat down, telling me to finish.

"You're really good," he said, and afterwards he

THE 'WHAT MIGHT HAVE BEEN' CHAPTER

approached me with his manager, asking if I'd be a rig in the audience, meaning he'd pick me out when he was handing the mic around, tell me how good I was and get me up on stage. They'd pay me £1,000 per show, but I was by then a football agent.

I explained what had happened with Mickie Most all those years back and that, in my eyes, that had been my chance gone. I was a football agent now but I thanked them for the offer. I still did the odd show here and there to help people out and keep my hand in, and in the mid-1990s I used to go up and sing four or five songs before the main act and nobody had a clue who I was. I went under the name 'Silky' and occasionally somebody would ask, "Are you that ex-footballer?" After that, I stopped doing session work and then stopped doing vocals altogether.

The sting in the tale for me is that the song that I had recorded for Mickie ended up being recorded and released by the guy who wrote it – Adrian Gurvitz (amazingly I met him for the first time in October 2024). It was called 'Classic' and it ended up being a huge hit in 1982 in the UK and overseas. He made a fortune from it, and I can only guess or dream what might have been. It wasn't meant to be.

I've been surrounded by showbiz folk for as long as I can remember and no doubt my early performances on stage with my mum as a kid was the root of a fascination with entertainment and entertaining. I even tried to be the entertainer on the football pitch so it was no surprise I suppose that I mixed more in showbiz circles than I did in football.

I became close to Bill Kenwright after I'd been invited to play in a Showbiz XI and I was only young at the time. That's where I first met Bill and it led to a lifelong friendship that only ended when we lost him in October 2023.

Bill was in Coronation Street every now and then at the time and he was playing in this team put together by Jess Conrad, and every now and then over a period of time we played matches that raised money for various charitable causes. Actors, singers, entertainers… it was a mix of celebrities and a few players (like me) who could play a bit and enjoyed meeting up. Chris Quinten, 'Diddy' David Hamilton, Kenny Lynch, Dennis Waterman… the list goes on.

After one game we were in the pub and the lead singer of a very famous rock band had been playing.

Let's just say he got no satisfaction from what Jess said, who was only having some lad banter when he said, "My god, your face is full of lines. You need some Oil of Olay, love."

The singer said, "These are laughter lines."

Jess, sharp as a tack, said, "Nothing's that fucking funny!"

THE 'WHAT MIGHT HAVE BEEN' CHAPTER

I remained close to Bill and knew him long before he became involved in football. It's funny in some ways that I brokered the last transfer deal of Bill's chairmanship with Demarai Gray's move to Saudi Arabia.

My last phone call with Bill was the night before his operation. I was under the impression he was to have a major procedure on the Monday morning, so I sent him a text saying, 'Good luck BK, I'm sure everything will be fine, and we'll be speaking again soon.'

On that same Monday evening, my phone rang, and it was a withheld number – and though I don't usually answer withheld numbers, I did on this occasion. It was Bill. He said, "Silks?"

I said, "BK… that was quick. How did the operation go?"

He told me the op was the next morning, not that day as I'd thought. He said, "Whatever you do, don't forget about Demarai Gray", and I told him not to worry and that everything was going through smoothly.

He said, "Good – if there's anyone who can get that deal done, it's you." Then he said, "Silks, the op tomorrow… it's a big one."

I said, "BK, you're gonna be fine and you'll come through this."

He said, "Silks, I want to tell you something."

"What's that?" I asked.

"I love you."

I said, "I love you too, BK, and we'll talk again in a few weeks."

But we never did. He died some days later having never recovered from that major operation he'd undergone, and I miss him so much because we used to talk all the time. He loved Everton Football Club with all his heart, but even though he was caught up in all the fan protests and criticism over the years, he was just the chairman – he didn't own the club and it wasn't him putting money in. He knew all that so everything went over his head, but he would never come out and say that because he didn't want to criticise or upset anyone. He was a warm, lovely guy.

So, it was showbiz all the way for me and a lot of the people I was close to in football had showbiz connections.

I met a lot of stars because of my friendship with George Best. Billy Connolly and I became friends, and my life revolved around the entertainment world.

We'd been on nodding terms over the years, but I remember George coming up to me at a party and saying, "All these women I speak to keep saying 'Silky this or Silky that', so I thought 'I've got to meet this guy'," and we hit it off and he invited me to several parties, and we stayed in touch.

When I first met George, he was married to Mary Stavin who had been Miss World, and later Angie Best.

THE 'WHAT MIGHT HAVE BEEN' CHAPTER

I met more and more people at the parties George invited me to and I lost count of the amount of famous singers and actors I met over the years.

I would regularly see George and when I was playing for City, he called me one time and said, "Silks, we've got a great birthday party next week for Billy Connolly and everyone is going to be there."

I said it sounded great but there was no way I'd be able to get to London and George said, "No, it's going to be in Manchester at Sandpipers in Fallowfield."

I went along to the party which was full of very beautiful girls and George and I were in heaven! There were a few famous faces there, but it wasn't a major bash as such. I saw Billy and he was sweating buckets. I asked George if Billy was okay because he was dripping sweat off his forehead and didn't look so good. George said, "Funnily enough, I was thinking the same thing!"

I asked George to ask him if he was okay and he said, "No way – you've got a lot more front than I have, you ask him." So I did. I went over to Billy and said, "Are you okay, Billy?"

He said, "Hi Silks, yeah I'm great thanks."

I said, "It's just you're sweating like mad, and your shirt is drenched."

He was wearing this huge coat, and he just got up, took it off and handed it to me. As he did, I dropped it to the floor because of the weight. It weighed a tonne!

I said, "What the fuck is that?"

He said, "I've got all lead in it. I needed to lose about two stone because I've got a massive tour coming up. I don't get time to exercise so the only way I could do it was to get this jacket made and the weight's been dropping off me. I've lost the two stone because I've sweated it out and this is probably the last time I'll need to wear it."

I'd never heard of that before and never heard of it since, but it worked!

Another good showbiz pal is the guy everyone knows as Billy Ocean – but he's plain old Les Charles to me and I'd like to think I helped more than a little bit in bringing him to the attention of the wider world.

There was a record shop called Wally For Wireless on the Whitechapel Market and we used go there – me and some of my mates – and play records in the shop and Les, who was a couple of years older than me, was one of the guys who would regularly be in there.

Les was singing part-time and working in the day, and a friend of mine called Martin Jay was told by a producer called Lawrence Joseph – Lawrie J to everyone – to look for a singer. Martin said that he knew somebody who sang at the Streatham Locarno, which was an old music and dancehall.

Martin asked Lawrie why he wanted a singer and he said he had a gig at a recording studio to record three

THE 'WHAT MIGHT HAVE BEEN' CHAPTER

songs and he had a Scottish singer who had dropped out at the last minute.

Martin told him to go and listen to Les sing at the Locarno and see what he thought because he was definitely good enough according to my testimonials.

Lawrie J went along, liked what he heard and went in the studio and recorded three songs with Les, but none of them did anything.

He told Les, "You know what we've got to do? We've got to change your name."

So he did. He went in the studio one day as Les Charles and came out as Billy Ocean. They re-released the first song under the new name and 'Love Really Hurts Without You' took off and went to No.2 in the UK and made the top 30 in the USA. The rest, as they say, is history!

Chapter 13

GONE TO THE DOGS?

I'd been dabbling here and there after my time with Crewe, still not really sure where the next chapter lay.

I had a pet greyhound for about a year, and he'd previously been a racer in his time but was in retirement now.

One day, I got a call out of the blue from a guy called Tom Stanley, who I knew from my many visits to White City, and he asked me why I didn't get a licence and get my dog racing again. I said he hadn't raced for more than a year and I wouldn't even know where to start when it came to training him and he just said that I should do it the same as football training. Lots of gallops, long walks, sprinting, long distances, short distances, some days harder than others – all that plus a good diet. So I did. I applied for an owner/trainer licence and gave it a go. I had nothing to lose and not much else to do!

I took my dog to the beach at Southend to run, fed him a good mixed diet with plenty of fresh meat from the butchers, vegetables, wholemeal bread, cornflakes in the morning, brewers yeast, royal jelly, ginseng, and he just got fitter, leaner and quicker. It would be a pattern I followed with each and every dog I ended up working with. They were undoubtedly eating better than I was!

When he was what I considered up to a good standard, I put him back on the track. He had to be trialled first to check he was in good condition and when he'd more than proved he was, he was allowed to race again, and on his first time out since retiring, he won at Ipswich. And then he won his second and third races, too.

I thought maybe there might be something in this, so I bought another dog called Waiiea Flash.

He'd never won a race in his life and was always coming in the last two places, but I fell in love with him, so I bought him for £1,200. Everyone thought I was mad because his true worth was probably more like £500, but like footballers, I could see enough in him to believe he could be something special and trained him as well. He improved 20 lengths in pace in the time that I trained him and was soon running like a world beater. He was doing so well, I received an offer from a guy in America for £40,000!

I didn't take it because the dog had become my pet and was living in my house, but almost overnight, it seemed like I was fielding call after call from people wanting me to train their dogs. I'd somehow become a self-taught greyhound trainer, and a pretty successful one at that.

My average for the dogs I trained was between 10 and 15 lengths improvement, but maybe because I'd come into the game with no real experience, I was doing things my way with gut instinct instead of the tried and tested methods. Of course, I spoke to other trainers along the way and picked up tips here and there, but I'd found – or stumbled – on a formula that worked.

The average for most trainers was to have around 80 dogs in their stable, so to speak, but at my busiest I only had eight – yet I still ended up in the top six in the trainer's championship after winning about 90 races. It was unbelievable, really, particularly for somebody with no real history of dog training.

I trained dogs for other people too, and had some good owners – as well as some shit ones. I had one dog

I was convinced was going to win one race and told the owner to back him heavily – which he did – and he ended up winning £25,000. My thanks? A £40 tip. Yep, £40.

I won another big competition at Wembley, the Trafalgar Cup, which was a really big deal in dog racing with a greyhound called Maddison Supreme. The owner – a German guy called Johan – pocketed about £30,000 in prize money and bets, but not only did he not treat me to anything, he came to the kennels the next day when I was out, took the dog and didn't even pay the kennel bill he owed!

I was living in a small village called Canewdon at the time with my long-time girlfriend Mandy.

I'd been with her 14 years, and we'd been through a lot together, but after initially being around all the time after my football career ended, the dog training and success I was having meant I was spending more and more time away from home and as a result, we started to drift apart.

It was a real shame, but it was an amicable parting and I'll always have very fond memories of my time with her because she was a lovely girl. I'm happy that she met somebody, got married, and had a child because she deserves to be happy.

My passion for football may have dimmed, but the game was still in my blood, and I still played every weekend at amateur level to keep fit and just for the enjoyment more than anything else.

In 1987, an old mate of mine, Alan Gane, was manager of Wycombe Wanderers who were in the Isthmian League at the time. He asked if I felt fit and whether I would go and play for Wycombe for a few games as he thought my experience would be good for the rest of his players. I agreed and would end up playing just eight matches for them, but the last one against Tooting had a caveat to it. I told Alan I had would have to come off at 4.25pm as one of my dogs was racing that evening so I'd need to beat the crowd leaving the stadium.

I remember nonchalantly flicking the ball across goal from a corner for a team-mate to tap home and after a quick celebration, my number went up to come off, and I made the race in good time! I must have made a decent impression because years later, I was told I'd been named in a fan poll for the best Wycombe Wanderers team of all time. After eight games!

Not long after, another mate of mine had called me. He was the manager of Chelmsford City. He called to see if I could help them out and said I'd be the best player at the club. Flattery was going to get him everywhere! I was a free agent so I could play for anyone I wanted, but after a couple of games, the standard was so poor I had to tell them it just wasn't for me.

GONE TO THE DOGS?

So, aged 36, I decided that was probably it and packed it in altogether. Only I didn't quite finish completely, as I would later turn out for Wingate & Finchley, where I'd play for a couple of seasons and really enjoyed it, but I had by then become a football agent — more of that shortly — and it was taking up too much of my time.

Finally, I was asked to turn out for Harrow Borough in 2000 — by now 48 years old — to see if, again, I could help them out for a few games.

They'd made it to the FA Cup first round proper and they wanted me to be on the bench for the game away to my old club Wycombe Wanderers, who were now a league club. How could I say no? We were 3-0 down at Adams Park when I came on with 75 minutes on the clock — and I would later be told I was the oldest player to play in the FA Cup since Sir Stanley Matthews had turned out in the 1960s.

I wasn't on long, but — even if I do say so myself — I was having a blinder and I'll never forget their manager, Lawrie Sanchez, getting up off his bench and shouting, "Can someone kick that fucking old cunt?"

I looked over at Lawrie and shouted back, "Not so much of the old, please Lawrie."

So, I'd been doing this and that, trying my hand here and there and just bobbing along when, in 1993, an unexpected opportunity fell into my lap, and it was one that would change my life completely. I was 41 by this point, still training greyhounds and still very successful in my new profession. The only problem was, I wasn't making any money and was basically skint.

But all that was about to change…

Chapter 14

BARRY SILKMAN: FOOTBALL AGENT

Given my contacts in the game and eye for talent, maybe becoming a football agent was always my destiny, but it wasn't a job I'd ever imagined I'd end up doing.

And just like greyhound training, I sort of fell into it, had early success, and carried on from there. But the truth is, I hadn't a clue what I was doing!

It all started in 1993 when I got a call out of the blue from a lad called Danny O'Shea, who I'd played with at Southend United and was now at Cambridge

United. He asked me if I thought I could help a team-mate of his called Alan Kimble – an experienced left-back – find a new club. All told, I had been out of the game for about five years, and I didn't really watch any football either, so I told him I'd lost touch with any contacts that I might have had. Danny insisted all the same people were still involved, so maybe I wasn't as out of touch with everything as I thought. He insisted that I knew 'everyone in football' so asked if I would give it a go.

Danny was convinced Kimble was a good player and asked me to go and watch him play, so I said I would. Three weeks passed and I hadn't got around to it, so Danny called me again and said he would leave me a ticket at reception and asked me to get down and watch him that evening if I could. I had no dogs racing that night, so I went. I watched the match and thought Kimble was a decent player – not my sort of player – but he was strong, could ping long balls to feet and had good pace. He wasn't cultured, but effective with what he did.

I told Danny I had liked what I had seen and that he had some good attributes, so he asked me if I could find him a new club. I said I would try but left it there. I wasn't an agent, and I wouldn't have a clue where to begin.

In fact, I'd driven to Cambridge in my old van that

I transported my dogs around with and now I was agreeing to try and broker a deal with a Premier League club. Looking from the outside in, people might have suggested I needed a reality check, but the fact was, I love helping people and Danny had such faith in me. I felt obliged to at least give it a go, so I did. A week or so later, Danny called me.

It was late April, and the end of the season was fast approaching, and he said, "Silks, have you found a club for Kimbo yet?" I told him I hadn't, but I hadn't even tried by that point, mostly because I hadn't had a clue where to start.

This particular Saturday, I had no dogs racing anywhere, which was really rare as usually that was my biggest night, so I decided to watch Match of the Day for the first time in a long time.

One of the games featured Wimbledon and I didn't enjoy it all, but what immediately jumped out was that they were playing the same style Alan Kimble had played when I went to watch him. They were just knocking the ball long up to the big No.9 and then picking up his knockdowns.

Afterwards, they interviewed the Wimbledon manager Joe Kinnear, and I thought, "Fuck me, Joe Kinnear, manager of Wimbledon?" I'd known Joe for years, but only as a player and later as an assistant to Dave Mackay. During the interview, he said that he had just sold their left-back – Terry Phelan – to Manchester City and he was on the lookout for a new one. It felt almost like fate was playing a hand in my future as there had been too many coincidences in a short period of time.

So, on the Monday morning, I phoned the Wimbledon training ground and asked if I could speak with Joe Kinnear. They asked who was calling and I said, "Just tell him it's Silky."

A few seconds later, Joe came on the line. "Silky – that's weird, I was going to call you!"

I said, "Really? Why's that JK?"

He told me it was because he had just bought a greyhound and he'd heard I was a trainer now and wanted me to train his dog.

I said, "Fuck the greyhound, I've got a left-back you should sign."

He asked who it was, and I told him.

"Yeah," he said, "I know about him. We've had reports and the verdict was he's not good enough."

"Trust me," I said, "he's exactly what you need."

He told me they didn't have much money to spend, but he agreed to come and watch him play the following week. In between, a van turns up at my house with a greyhound and the guy says that Joe Kinnear wants me to train his dog. Terrific!

I called Joe and asked if he'd seen Alan Kimble play yet and he said he hadn't. Cambridge had one game left, and it had plenty riding on it. They were away to West Ham and if they lost, they would go down to the third tier, while West Ham needed a win to get promoted to the Premier League.

Wimbledon weren't playing that day, so I said to take the owner, Sam Hammam, with him and watch Kimble play. He agreed and they went along as planned. West Ham won 2-0, meaning Kimble was now a League One player.

Joe called me on the following Monday and said, "You know Silks, I quite like him. Can you get him for less than £300,000?"

I said I was certain I could – but it was just bluster because I still didn't have a clue where to start.

"Okay, go and do the deal," said Joe.

I called Danny up and asked who the Cambridge manager was and asked what his number was. He told me his gaffer was Gary Johnson. I had a plan – of sorts! I called the number, and a voice answered that I recognised. I said, "I know that voice, who is it?"

He said, "I know your voice – who's that?"

I said, "Well who is it, then?"

He said, "Tell me who you are first."

I said, "It's Silks."

He replied, "Fuck me, Silks. It's Griff."

'Griff' was Johnny Griffin, the former chief scout at Crystal Palace and somebody I'd known for years.

When I was at QPR, he lived about four doors away from me and we'd spend many afternoons in each other's houses just talking about football. He'd also been a part-time cab driver, and I assumed he'd drifted out of the game.

"Fuck me, Griff – what are you doing at Cambridge?" It turned out that the manager was his son-in-law!

He asked me how the greyhounds were going, and I explained that it had gone really well, but that I wasn't making a penny from it. I then said, "Griff, I need you to do me a favour. I need you to tell me that Alan Kimble can be sold for less than £300,000."

He asked why and I told him the story of how it had got to this stage, and he told me to leave it with him. He said, "I'll tell you what, Silks – I'll tell Gary to sell him for £270,000."

Being an agent couldn't be as easy as that, could it?

I got off the phone and then called Joe Kinnear and said, "Joe, I can get him for £270,000."

He said, "Great, what salary are you looking at for him?"

Again, I hadn't a clue and told him so. He just laughed and told me to come into his office as soon as I could. I did, and when I got there, Joe had spread all the contracts of his players out on the desk and said I should take a look at all of them and figure out what I thought was a decent wage.

By the time I'd finished, I said, "The average is about £1,200, Joe."

He said, "Okay, I'll give him £1,400 plus £200 appearance fee."

I called Alan Kimble, and he couldn't believe it. He was absolutely ecstatic. "You're fucking joking, aren't you?"

And that was that. We did the deal, I think I made £2,500 from that transfer in commission which, again, I guessed at, and later I would learn it was a fraction of what an agent usually made. The first thing I did was go to a friend's car dealership and chose a smart looking car for £4,000 – my dealer mate told me he'd do it for £2,500 and I bought it with the money I'd been paid for Kimble. I couldn't really be representing footballers in a van I transported dogs around in, could I?

I thought about how it had all happened, how many coincidences and breaks I'd had along the way. The stars had all aligned at just the right time and I felt there had been more than a touch of fate about it all.

Prior to all this, I'd met the love of my life, Alison – Ally – who I'd met when I answered a plea for help from a single mother of a disabled baby girl.

She lived in the same village as a friend of mine, and I'd spotted the article in a local newspaper after I'd stayed over and couldn't get to sleep. She was asking for people to help her and her daughter – volunteers who could help her cope with one or two things – so I offered my time in between training dogs.

I did what I could, fell in love with Ally's little baby and eventually, fell in love with Ally. She was my soulmate, and we were soon married, and I adopted her daughter.

We didn't have any money, but we were deeply in love and incredibly happy.

Ally was my rock, and I wondered how I'd ever got by without her.

It was Ally who encouraged me to become a full-time football agent, but I told her most players already had agents – and experienced ones at that. She said that Alan Kimble hadn't, and I agreed there might be an opportunity, or that it was at worst worth giving it a go.

As much as I enjoyed training dogs, I was never going to be wealthy doing it, so why not? I had plenty of connections in the game and even if I didn't know literally everyone in football, as Danny O'Shea had suggested, it turned out I knew a lot of them. It had felt like destiny had played a hand in everything up to that point, so I decided I'd give it a go.

It was another case of 'What is the worst that could happen?'

Chapter 15

A GENT AND AN AGENT

Ally proved to be the driving force behind me becoming an agent.

She contacted the Football Association to get the ball rolling and they told me that I would have to sit an exam with an interview first.

At that time, a lot of people knew me and knew that I'd been a player at Palace, City and QPR, and also been an assistant manager at Orient, so when I went to be interviewed by the FA panel, they ended up just talking to me about football. What was it like working under Terry Venables? What was the difference in coaching styles between Terry and Malcolm Allison? We spoke about football and nothing else for about an hour-and-a-half and at the end, they said, "Look, it's an absolute waste of time you taking an exam, you know football inside out, whereas most of the licensed agents are businessmen – at least you'll be able to give footballers the right advice, so we're happy to approve your application to start operating."

That was it. I was now a FIFA-registered agent with a licence number of S123 – it could have been my car reg! I had to have a photo taken for the picture on the licence and I was wearing a Sporting Lisbon shirt that a player had given me a few years back. There can't have been many agents who had their official picture taken wearing a football shirt, I'm guessing, but I'd always been a 'what you see is what you get' sort.

I was up and running and soon brokering deals here and there. Alan Kimble had recommended me to a couple of players who didn't have any representation, so I took them on, but it was very much a case of learning as I went along. I was working from my office at home and Ally was my secretary/chief of admin.

You're never sure how it will all progress when you start anything like this. I knew I was well connected and that it might take time to build up a list of clients, but I was surprised just how quickly things started to happen.

Not long after I'd officially started, I got a call from a

guy called Tom Somani, who said he knew a guy who knew me and heard I had recently become a FIFA-registered agent. He told me he worked for the Australian Institute for Sport (AIS) and that he'd been told I was a really good judge of players and that he had three teenagers he wanted me to help get trials with a view to joining English clubs. Tom promised they were really good but, as ever, I'd want to see them play for myself before passing judgement. If I started recommending players I'd never seen and even one or two turned out to be duds, my reputation – such as it was at that point – would soon suffer.

I spoke with Ray Wilkins at Queens Park Rangers and then told Tom I'd get all three lads a two-week trial during pre-season. We set the ball rolling for dates and travel arrangements and a few weeks later I met them at the airport, but it turned out only two had travelled so I phoned Tom and asked where the other lad was.

He said the other lad had an agent called Archie Blue who he sometimes dealt with and between Tom and Archie, they'd decided the lad wasn't strong enough physically – a bit lightweight, in fact – to take on the challenge of men's football in England. He was also only 15, but Archie would bring the lad over not long after for a trial with Leeds United, who took him on. His name was Harry Kewell.

Ray Wilkins had Billy Bonds and John Hollins

helping him at QPR – not a bad trio! I took the other two lads there for their trial. They were called Andrew McDermott and Lucas Neill, and I went along to watch them in training.

I then went to see a pre-season friendly at Stevenage and McDermott started, but Neill was on the bench. I thought McDermott had a big chance and Neill came on in the second half, made a few mistakes but then did some tremendous things – great runs, movement, and intelligent positional play. I absolutely loved what I'd seen and thought Neill was actually better than McDermott.

At the end of the game, I spoke with Ray. He told me they really liked McDermott and wanted to sign him, but they thought Neill wasn't going to make it. Ray said, "Chris Gieler, our chief scout, plus John and Billy think he's got no chance, Silks. I'm not that adamant he won't make it, so can we keep him for another two weeks to make a fuller judgement?"

I said, "Ray, that can't happen because he has to be back at the AIS on Monday to start school again. Those three (Billy, John and Chris) are so wrong. This kid is an absolute certainty."

Ray said he'd only played 20 minutes and asked how I could be so sure. I told him I didn't care if he'd played five – I'd seen enough ability in that time to know he was nailed on to make it.

A GENT AND AN AGENT

Ultimately, they decided not to take him and after calling his father to tell him they weren't going to offer him a contract, he went back to Australia as planned with McDermott, who would return to sign for QPR a week later. I thought that was that. Three days later, Lucas Neill's father called me and asked if I could get his son to England.

I asked why and he told me Lucas was going to be kicked out of the Australian Institute for Sport for disciplinary reasons and if that happened he said no club in Australia would touch him because the AIS would have to state why he had been kicked out.

I told him I thought Lucas had what it took to make it and that he should leave it with me. I had a great relationship with Millwall chairman Reg Burn at the time and also with their manager Mick McCarthy, so I arranged an urgent meeting with them both.

I said to them, "How much do you trust me? You've known me long enough to know what a good judge of a player I am, so do you trust me enough to give this kid a three-year contract without seeing him play and on my word alone? It's going to cost you a couple of thousand, but I don't even think you'll have to pay that, and you'll get him for free. He's been at QPR, and they didn't want him, but they've made a massive mistake."

Reg said, "How much do you want?"

I said, "Nothing – just sign him. But once you see how good he is and offer him an improved contract, that's when you can really look after me."

Reg said that sounded more than fair and they agreed to take him on. I got him a good deal then called his father who couldn't believe it and Lucas signed for the club. He was a central midfielder, 18, and in his first youth game against Leyton Orient he absolutely destroyed them. He then played a few reserve games and within a few weeks, McCarthy put him straight into the first team.

Reg paid me 10 grand for the deal, but I spent it all buying Lucas furnishings and kitchenware for his apartment, so technically, I'd not made a penny on the deal, but I was fine with that because I knew that when his contract was renegotiated – which it would be fairly quickly – I'd earn a decent commission.

In fact, not long after, Reg called me up and said, "Barry, you're about to make yourself a lot of money. I want to do a new contract with Lucas, and I want you to sort it all out by next week."

Millwall and Reg had been as good as their word – but I was about to learn than being a football agent was a ruthless business as I was stabbed in the back by Lucas Neill and his dad.

I would never get a penny from the vastly improved contract Millwall had offered because Reg called me

A GENT AND AN AGENT

later that day to say Lucas had told him he no longer wanted me as his representative and had found somebody else to represent him.

I couldn't believe it. Lucas would have had no football career without my intervention, and I was fuming – not so much because of the money, just because they hadn't done the decent thing. Lucas went on to play for Blackburn Rovers, West Ham, and Everton, winning almost 100 caps for his country, but that was the thanks I got.

As for Andrew McDermott, he only played a few games for QPR before moving on to West Brom for £450,000, but his baby daughter became ill and he had to return to Australia and his career sort of petered out after that, which was a shame for the lad.

As a result of those two deals, I started getting a load of Australian players on my books, simply through word of mouth, but I still didn't have a clue what to charge for my cut each time they signed for a club.

My first six deals should have made me around £300,000, but I earned £30,000 because my rates were so low.

I was soon travelling the world watching players, signing them up and finding them clubs in England. I was earning a good reputation for finding quality, and managers and chairmen were starting to trust me.

Another of my early deals involved Republic of

Ireland winger Mark Kennedy and I helped save Millwall from going out of business in the process.

It was March 1995, and I was sitting with Millwall chairman Reg Burr in his office who had told me the club would be wound up at the end of the week unless they could raise £500,000.

I said, "Reg, is there any player any clubs have shown interest in?"

He said, "Yeah, Liverpool like Mark Kennedy but they're not making a decision until the end of the season."

I told Reg to leave it with me. I called Ray Harford up at Blackburn. He was a great friend of mine and had taken over as manager from Kenny Dalglish. Rovers and Liverpool were big rivals at the time so there was an edge.

I told Ray that I needed a massive favour.

I asked him to send a fax over to Reg Burr saying that Rovers wanted to buy Mark Kennedy for £1 million, which would be paid in one go and to add they wanted Mark up for a medical to get the deal done. Within 15 minutes he'd sent the fax.

Then I called Liverpool chief executive Peter Robinson and told them I knew they were interested in Mark Kennedy but didn't intend to make a decision on him until the summer. Robinson admitted they really liked him, but agreed they weren't looking to clinch a deal at the moment.

A GENT AND AN AGENT

I told him he would be too late if he waited because Blackburn had just faxed an offer over for Kennedy and it was sat in the in-tray waiting for him.

I said, "I'm sat in Reg's office, but he's nipped out and hasn't see it yet."

He asked if I could send the fax over to him with the details on. Robinson asked me to then hide it, get rid of it or whatever while he looked over Rovers' offer. Within half an hour, he'd sent an offer by fax and Reg accepted it immediately and got the £1milllion the club needed.

I suppose I was a little economical with the truth, but I was just forcing Liverpool's hand. They probably would have come back with an offer in a few months anyway, but Millwall would have gone under by then.

The club was saved, Kennedy had a dream move, and everyone was happy – except me. Because I was still learning the ropes, I hadn't put an agreement in place for my commission.

I should have told Reg that if I got a deal done, anything over the £500,000 they needed to survive, we'd split 50/50 – that would have been £250,000 each – but I didn't get anything down on paper for facilitating the deal and any commission was at Reg's discretion.

He ended up paying me £5,000! It wasn't the first time Reg took the piss either as he'd pulled a similar trick when I got Kenny Cunningham and Jon Goodman to Wimbledon for him at a cost of £1.2m. So after the Kennedy deal, I told him thanks but no thanks and never worked with him again.

That's why I always smile when people assume football agents make fortunes. I missed out on lot of money with a number of those early deals and I definitely didn't make fortunes – certainly not where Reg Burr was concerned anyway!

I took a player to Derby County on one occasion when Jim Smith was manager and he called his assistant, Steve McClaren, over to come and meet me at the hotel I was brokering the deal at.

Jim said to Steve, "Do you know who this is? This is Barry Silkman – we call him Silky – and he is the best judge of a footballer you will ever meet. If you ever become a manager and he tells you to buy a player, don't check your scout reports, question him, or hesitate; just buy the player. If he says he has a player you might want to take a look at, it's because he is good enough, but he's not sure whether he will suit your style of play."

A couple of years later, Steve took over at Middlesbrough where I already had one of my players – goalkeeper Mark Schwarzer. Steve called me and said, "I've never forgotten what Jim said to me about you and I want you to help me put a team together."

So I found him six or seven players that would eventually help Middlesbrough get to the UEFA Cup final in their most successful spell ever with a team mostly made up of players I'd found for him. Ugo Ehiogu, Doriva, Yakubu, Franck Queudrue, George Boateng – nearly the whole starting XI!

Doriva had been with Celta Vigo, but they weren't playing him because if he made one more appearance, they'd have to give him an agreed amount of money, which they weren't prepared to do. I told Steve Gibson, the chairman, "Take him until the end of the season – he's on £15k per week but will take £1k a week and £10k appearance money and a place to live. I don't want a penny – just get him over and see how good he is."

He came over, played about 10 games before the end of the season and they loved him. They offered him a three-year deal and he was brilliant, winning the Middlesbrough Players' Player of the Year award for two years running. I had found my niche and was loving it.

Chapter 16

COULDA, WOULDA, SHOULDA!

As far as me being a football agent went, things were going well.

I'd get recommendations from all over the world, go and watch players and if I liked them, take them on board. Because I'd always loved assessing and I'd always trusted my own eyes more than anyone else's, I had probably found my ideal job. I'd done that throughout my life as soon as I'd got into football professionally – only now I got paid for it as well. Today, players are assessed by computers, stats and data and I'd back myself against that process every day of the week, because what that method doesn't tell you is the information you can't crunch into numbers and percentages. Did the player make the right move previously? What is he like as a person? What is going on in the background? None of that will show up in a statistician's report.

That was my strength, and I was now making a good living out of it.

But there are plenty of tales of what could have been, what should have been and what didn't happen along the way when it comes to trying to place players at certain clubs – including some that will leave you scratching your head.

Some of the players involved went on to become world superstars, but at the time of the proposed deals, they weren't that well known, meaning clubs could have bought multi-million pound talent for peanuts.

Here are some of the best...

I was alerted to the talents of a 24-year-old attacking midfielder at Bordeaux and went along to watch him. His name was Zinedine Zidane, and it took me about five minutes to decide that this guy was going to be something very special.

I had brought a number of good players to Newcastle United under Kevin Keegan's reign and every one of them was a success, so Zidane felt like the perfect fit for a Keegan team.

It was 7 January, 1996, and I told Kevin he could sign Zidane for £1.2million – it was a steal. I begged Kevin to sign him, but in the end he told me his chief scout thought he wasn't good enough and years later, Kevin told me he should have listened to me instead of his scout.

Zidane eventually signed for Juventus and the rest is history.

More than 20 years later, Kevin would tell me I was the best agent he ever came across – the only good one in his opinion. Nice words from a top man who I always got along really well with over the years.

I wish I'd kept the fax that was sent on to me from Newcastle United where the chief scout stated, 'Silky has grossly overrated the player. At best he is good enough for Wolves who are bottom of the Championship at present.'

I think Zidane was slightly better than the players in a struggling Wolves team!

When I had watched Zinedine play at Bordeaux, another player – the Bordeaux left-back – caught my eye and impressed me so much. I agreed with the club that I would get them £800,000 by finding him an English club. They said I would get 10% of the fee up to £800k and 50% for anything above that.

About a week later I got a call from David Pleat, who was manager of Sheffield Wednesday at the time, and he asked me what I thought of Ben Thatcher, who was playing for Wimbledon.

I said, "He's got limitations, gives away too many free-kicks, and I don't think he'll take you where you want to go. He's not a terrible player, don't get me wrong, but he can only do so much."

Pleat said, "Yeah, but I like him."

I said, "If you are after a new left-back, I can do a deal for you with a French player called Bixente Lizarazu and it will cost you £800,000. He's absolutely brilliant."

He said, "Oh yes, I've heard of him, but he's too small."

I said, "Dave, what do you want, a footballer or a basketball player? What does his size have to do with anything? I'm telling you, he will become one of the top four left-backs in the world."

But he didn't take him because he wanted Ben Thatcher, who eventually went to Tottenham in the end, and, ironically, played under Dave Pleat for a short time. Ben made a good career for himself, but he always had the moment of madness in him as he demonstrated with that outrageously bad challenge on Portsmouth's Pedro Mendes while with Manchester City.

One manager I never had the pleasure of dealing with was Brian Clough, but like anyone who has been in football a long time, you hear one or two stories about Old Big 'Ead – and they never disappoint!

A mate of mine called Ron Howell was at Brighton when Cloughie took over and at the first training session he took, Ron got the ball on the halfway line and knocked it through Cloughie's legs. He immediately blew the whistle he had hanging around his neck and went up to Ron. He pointed to the ball. "You see this, son?" Then he pointed to his head. "You see this, son?" Then he pointed down to his feet. "You see those, son? Forty goals a season for four years running – not fucking nutmegs on the halfway line. Now fuck off, because you'll never play for this club again."

Ron laughed, thinking he was joking, but he could soon tell he was doing anything but. That was that. Ron was gone inside a week.

Another time, one of my players – Mark Crossley – recalled a hilarious story when he played for Clough at Nottingham Forest.

Cross had just broken into the first team at Forest but was still commuting from South Yorkshire. After a 3-2 win over Coventry, he said goodbye to the lads and that he'd see them on Monday when Cloughie appeared. "Where do you think you're going young man?"

"Home, boss."

"Where's home?"

"Barnsley."

"Right," said Cloughie. "Tomorrow morning, my house at 9am and bring your boots. It would help if you brought your gloves as well."

Cross hadn't a clue where Cloughie lived or why he wanted him to go to his home or what he had planned for him. After enlisting the help of the groundsman, he turned up on time at his house and knocked on the door. Cloughie's wife Barbara answered and invited him in, saying Brian would be down in a moment.

She made him a cup of tea and a slice of toast when Brian finally appeared.

He said, "I won't call you shit-house (his nickname for Cross) because Barbara's here. I want to thank you for turning up on time."

He then proceeded to tell him his son Simon was manager of a side in the Derbyshire Sunday League, and they didn't have a goalie.

"Thank you for agreeing to play for my son's team. They haven't got a goalkeeper, and I thought you'd do."

Cross played, but the other team found out who he really was (not the name submitted to the ref) and the club were fined £50 – all of which came out of Mark's wages when Cloughie docked his weekly Forest pay packet.

What a character. I wish I'd have met him or had the chance to play for him. It would never have been dull, I'm certain of that.

There were many more deals that could have happened, but didn't, and obviously that comes with the territory, but of all the managers I ever dealt with, one remains a complete mystery. I played alongside George Graham when I was at Crystal Palace and it makes me smile that he ended up such a strict disciplinarian given how he was as a player!

When I joined Palace, George was coming towards the end of his playing career and Terry Venables said he wanted me to share rooms with George for away games, which I didn't have a problem with. On one of our first trips as roommates, we arrived on the Friday evening ahead of the game the next day. Once we arrived at the hotel, George said, "Silks, we're on the first floor but we need a room on the ground because I've got a bird coming later and I'll have to climb out of the window."

So, I went down to reception and got the receptionist to get us a ground floor room, before telling TV that we'd changed for one reason or another. Later, we all had dinner together and went back to our rooms. Then George says, "Silks, whatever you do, don't fall asleep or else I won't be able to get back in."

I stayed up watching television until late and then I must have fallen asleep, only to be woken by this thumping on the window, well past midnight. George had returned from his rendezvous and in the years to come, I'd tell the story and then ask the question of how George ever became such a strict manager. Maybe it was because he knew as well as anyone what footballers would get up to given the chance. But the odd thing was, throughout his long management career, mainly at Arsenal, Leeds United and Tottenham, George never took one player I offered him – not one.

It was inexplicable. We knew each other well, got on well and he knew I could spot a player, but he wouldn't do a single deal with any of the lads I presented – and there were some top, top players, too.

Years later, he would be banned by the FA after it was found that he had accepted an illegal payment from agent Rune Hauge. All I can say is he seemed to do most of his business with Hauge.

It was so bad that, to test the water, I'd occasionally offer George players that weren't even available. They'd be worth £12million or more and weren't for sale, but I'd offer them to George for £4million and he still wouldn't take them. I saw him a few years back and I said, "George, any chance of buying a player off me?" He said, "Silks, if I was a manager now, I would." I thought, "Yeah, I bet you fucking would, George!"

The bottom line is, I love George and have a lot of time for him, and always will.

I never really had any dealings with Manchester United during Alex Ferguson's reign, other than one that should never have happened. I played a role in Kleberson's move to Old Trafford, but it should never have happened because he wasn't at that level – one of very few regrets of mine as an agent. I never dealt with Ferguson as he didn't get involved with negotiations. It was always people like Ed Woodward who I spoke to and I always got on really well with him. Fergie was just there to make the players feel good and get the best out of them.

Regarding my old club, I took a Dutch lad called Gerard Wiekens to Manchester City. He would have made an outstanding holding midfielder in today's game, but back then it was either centre-back or midfielder – they didn't really have the pivot. If they had, he'd have been perfect because he was a quality footballer.

I also took a winger called Tony Scully to City, but it didn't really work out.

I did loads of deals with Harry Redknapp and had a good relationship with him, providing a number of players at the many clubs he ended up manager of. It's funny, though; sometimes it's the deals that didn't go through that you remember more and there was one with Harry regarding a Dutch right-back that even today I'm scratching my head about as I remember what actually happened.

The lad in question was a sure thing – a player who

would thrive in English football and I said, "H, I'll get him to you on a free transfer and he'll be the best player at the club."

He was about to play in the Dutch equivalent of the FA Cup final for Ajax, so I agreed to go with Harry to Amsterdam and watch him play.

"There's nothing not to like," I said, "And if you agree, he will meet us at the hotel the next morning at 6.30am and we can talk about putting a deal together."

Our flight was at 7.30am but our hotel was a two-minute walk from the terminal building, so we'd have 15 or 20 minutes to talk with him, which I knew would be more than enough.

So, we travelled to Holland and went to the stadium and there were scouts and agents everywhere – but they'd all come to watch a centre-half play. I saw Andy King from Everton and he said that his club were going to sign this centre-half, and I just said, "Andy, don't bother because he's joining to Juventus – and by the way, he's nowhere near fucking good enough."

He asked me who me and Harry had come to watch, so I told him, and he went, "Nah! You can't fancy him?"

He was so wrong, it was scary.

We watched the game, the lad we had come to see was excellent and Harry said, "Silks, let's do the deal. Get the player to our hotel in the morning and make sure he wants to come."

The next morning at half six, the player arrives bang on time, we have a coffee and H says, "Look, I desperately want you to come and play for me."

The lad says, "No problem – I'm coming."

The whole deal was done there and then and on the flight home, H tells me to go and see West Ham's chief executive, Peter Storrie, to sort the financials out. Two days later I hadn't heard a thing and the player was calling me to find out what was happening.

I called Storrie and he said, "Sorry Silks – Harry's changed his mind. He wants to take this right-back – Gary Charles – from Graeme Souness at Benfica instead.

I said, "Are you fucking kidding? He's useless!"

I called Harry and said, "What are you doing, H? Are you mad? This player I've found for you is five billion times better."

H was like, "Well, I'm not sure about him now…"

None of it made any sense.

Charles went to West Ham and, just like he'd been at Benfica, was injured all the time. He played eight games in four years. My player – the guy Harry had agreed to sign then changed his mind – went to Chelsea instead and didn't cost them a penny under the Bosman ruling. His name? Mario Melchiot. I think he went on to do pretty well at Stamford Bridge, if I'm not mistaken, while Charles was forced to retire, aged 32, due to the numerous injuries he'd sustained. Nothing personal against the lad and it wasn't his fault H got it wrong, which is something he didn't often do, in fairness.

I'd rate that deal falling through with Harry as one of my biggest disappointments in football because, as I say, it made no sense at all, and it has always been something of a mystery to me.

At that time, there was no way that deal couldn't get done unless Mario changed his mind in my opinion, yet Harry was the one who decided it wasn't going to happen and instead spends £5million on an injury-prone full-back who Souness was probably desperate to ship back to England. Every now and again, things in football make no sense, and this was one of them.

But while H made very few mistakes, another deal he did turned out badly – but that was my fault! It was a rare occasion where I misjudged a player – his name was Marco Boogers, who had a nightmare at West Ham, so after that, I told H, "We're even now!"

He missed a brilliant one and I introduced him to a duff one. It just goes to show, you should never pick Boogers!

There's one last Harry Redknapp story which still makes H and me laugh today.

I'd been informed of a player called Eyal Berkovic, who was owned by Maccabi Haifa in Israel but had spent the previous year on loan with Southampton. He was just the sort of exciting playmaker that West Ham needed.

I told H, who knew all about Eyal, and he asked me to help the move happen as he was exactly the sort of player he was looking for – and at £1.75million, he was definitely within budget.

We arranged for Eyal to fly back over to London, but along the way, Tottenham became aware of the deal and attempted to hijack it.

Eyal was brought to meet H and me, and we sold him on West Ham, but he was aware of the Tottenham interest and so wanted to speak with them as well, which made sense from his point of view.

Eyal made it clear that if he didn't like what Spurs had to say, he would sign for West Ham.

Meanwhile, Spurs chairman Alan Sugar called H and said something along the lines of 'why would he sign for West Ham when Spurs are interested?'

He was talking about how much bigger his club were, the obvious Jewish connection and was pretty much saying we should just withdraw to save embarrassment.

So, before Eyal left to go to White Hart Lane, I still had one ace up my sleeve.

Spurs were managed by Gerry Francis at the time – a guy I loved and had huge respect for, and still do – but Gerry has a habit of not looking in your eyes when he speaks.

It's just something he didn't do and was a natural way for him, but Eyal didn't know that.

So I said, "Eyal, Gerry is a top guy and a great manager, but if he really wants you, he will look you in the eye when he is talking. If he doesn't, it means he's not sure or doesn't really want to sign you."

Eyal nodded and said he'd let us know when the meeting had ended.

Later, he called back.

"Silky, you were right!" he said. "Not once did he look me in the eye, so I'm not signing for Spurs, I'll join West Ham."

I'd like to think if Alan Sugar had heard about this – which he still isn't aware of to this day (cat's out of the bag now!) – he might have said, "Silky, you're hired!"

The plan had worked perfectly, and West Ham United got a fantastic player for a couple of years before the bust-up with John Hartson.

Zidane to Newcastle and Lizarazu to Sheffield Wednesday were major disappointments, but the deals had never been agreed, whereas the Melchiot one had, and that's why it still rankles with me. I did plenty of business with H before and after that and have a great relationship with him to this day.

As a footnote to this story, Mario's team-mate – the one Andy King and all the other scouts had come to watch in Amsterdam that day – was called Sunday

Oliseh, a Nigerian centre-back. He did join Juventus, and he was useless I'm sorry to say.

Though I'd cite Lucas Neill as the exception to the rule, I never had a problem with players leaving me to take on other representation, though there haven't been many over the years. All they have to do is pick up the phone and let me know their intentions – that's all I ask.

Mark Schwarzer had been with me for many years when he called me one day and said he wanted to try another agent. I said, "Schwarzy, no problem."

He said, "What, are you alright with it? I thought you would go mad."

I said, "Look, you've been with me for 10 years – I've done fantastic for you, and you've done fantastic for me. If you want to try another agent in the latter stages of your career, I don't have a problem with that."

There are certain agents I didn't get on with and some I had major fallouts with – same with chairman and managers who only seem to want to use one company – but I've found that those clubs ultimately fail and as you never know when your paths might cross, I am not going to go into too much detail here.

On the family front, things were a bit of a struggle in my early days as an agent.

Ally, Danielle and me had lived in a rented shit-hole with no gas or cooker to begin with and I'd had to rig our electricity from an outside source in the street. We had nothing and it had taken me about five years to get to the stage where we were finally able to afford a home of our own, so I took things very personally.

We'd found a lovely house in Waltham Abbey, and it had been a hard slog to be in a position to buy it, but the night we moved in and a moment we should have been at our happiest, the bottom fell out of our world.

We had a friend of ours called Claire over, and Ally had put Danielle to bed for the night. She was aged five and was still severely disabled. Because we had no cooking facilities available at the time, I went out and got fish and chips for everyone and a bottle of champagne and orange juice to celebrate our first night there.

I got back, we put the food out and I filled the glasses to toast the house, but Ally said she'd go and check on Danielle before she ate. About 20 seconds later she screamed for me to come upstairs. I raced up and found Danielle with her head hanging over the side of the bed. I tried to give her the kiss of life, Ally called the paramedics who were there in minutes, but she was pronounced dead on arrival at hospital.

It was a complete and utter nightmare.

Our first night in the family home we dreamed of, and Danielle was gone. It was beyond our comprehension and for the first few months, we existed, but not much more.

We struggled on as best we could and eventually

decided to go to Mombasa for a break, and during our first stay we discovered these villages with kids that had very few possessions or decent clothes. Soon we decided to return and distribute Danielle's clothes to some of the village kids which was incredibly cathartic and heartrending.

Ally and I hadn't been intimate since Danielle's death, but after six months, during our second trip, we made love, and I told her that she would conceive and that we'd have a baby girl and that we would name her after the country she was conceived in. Eight weeks later, Ally told me she was pregnant and was expecting a girl. When she was born, we named her Keenia.

I had made a promise to my wife that we would never go through all that financial hardship and heartache again and I also told her that if anyone tried to take my living away from me, I would ruin them.

My mantra as a football agent has always been transparency and honesty. All I ever do is try to be fair to the player and the football club, but more and more my role has been to broker deals for clubs – be an intermediary who talks with all parties to try and find an acceptable deal.

In the summer of 2023, I brokered a deal on behalf of Everton for Demarai Gray to go and play in the Saudi Pro League. His agent is called Luca Bascherini, and I worked alongside him, kept him informed of what was happening and progressed a deal that way. Luca was acting on behalf of the player, and I was acting on behalf of Everton after Bill Kenwright asked me to find Demarai a new club, so that's what I did. I found him a club that met Everton's valuation and then Luca dealt with the club regarding Demarai's personal terms.

When everything was signed and sealed, I was paid a commission by Everton. It's a bit like selling a house – you have a buyer, you have a seller, and you have an intermediary working to bring both parties the solution they want. That's where I come in.

It's a specialised role and it means I approach clubs with players I believe – or know – might be available or about to become available who might suit their needs. That's how it starts, and you just move on from there.

With Lucas Paqueta, I spoke with West Ham chairman David Sullivan and told him I thought he needed a really top class midfielder and, with respect, getting top players to clubs like West Ham is not easy because they all want to play for Manchester City, United, Liverpool or Chelsea. But they are in London, have a fantastic stadium, a big fan base and have a chance to get someone in based on those factors alone.

I had a look around to see who was available and what might work when I got a call from a colleague in France who asked me if I knew of a player called

Lucas Paqueta. I said, "Yeah, he's Brazilian and a great player."

He told me Paqueta wasn't happy in France and there was a deal to be done. His agent was a father and son team, so I went to David and told him about Paqueta's possible availability, and he said that he had already been offered the player by Pini Zahavi, who was working for the father and son team. He said they wanted 50 million euros, which they couldn't afford. David asked me what I thought I could get Paqueta for and I said I thought I could get him for quite a bit less.

David said that if I could do that, I should sort the deal out and as he was going on holiday, to only contact him if it was absolutely necessary because he needed a break. That meant I had the authority to sort the transfer fee, the player's wages, and the agent's commission – in essence, I was to act as though I was West Ham United Football Club. I contacted the agent who was working on behalf of the club, Lille, and told them 50 million euros was a non-starter. In the end, I managed to get Paqueta for 35 million euros. There were a lot of bonuses included, but most of them are unlikely to ever happen – such as West Ham getting to the semi-final and final of the Champions League – and West Ham had a fantastic deal for a fantastic player, not to mention maybe £10-15k less per week in wage demands than they had originally been quoted. Ultimately, the transfer was fair to Paqueta, Lille and West Ham. David said, "Silks, you've done an unbelievable deal."

Negotiating is probably what I'm best at doing. I do deals where everyone is happy – or ones they can at least live with. Bill Kenwright had known me since I was 16 and he used to say I was the best 'deal getter' in the business, which is nice and there are plenty more who have told me the same.

Chapter 17

A LIGHT THAT NEVER GOES OUT

As good as being an agent was, I wasn't quite finished with the playing side of the game.

In 2018 my mate had helped out Staines Town FC financially and then sort of got lumbered with the club. He asked me if I could come and help for a few weeks as he had no manager, so I said I would.

He told me it would only be for a few weeks, so I said I'd go along and help out. I arrived and took part in my first training session and afterwards all the lads were saying I was the best player on the park which was worrying as I was 66! That was how bad it was. I took the club for three or four games until I got a letter from the FA saying they would be suspending my licence to be an agent because I couldn't do that and be a manager. I argued I was just helping my mate out with a club who attracted 250 people every week, but they wouldn't have it, so I had to tell my mate I couldn't do it any more. Ludicrous!

For some reason – and I still don't really know why to this day – Ally and I got divorced. That sounds a bizarre thing to say, but it's the truth. There was no reason I can put my finger on, but we separated and sort of went our own ways. I say sort of because we stayed best friends despite the split, and she still worked for me in an office at my house (for much of the time) as my PA. My life moved on, her life moved on, but we always remained close and, of course, we had Keenia, our daughter, to ensure that close bond was always there.

Eventually, Ally met a guy who was about 10 years younger than she was and he moved in with her after a while. I'd always looked after her financially, and when we divorced, she said, "Silk, I don't want half of your house and your money because you've worked so hard to get to where you are. I know you'll look after me and that's enough." And I did.

She told me that the day she didn't need my money, she would tell me and after about six months of living with her boyfriend, she called me to say that she didn't need any financial support any more. I pointed out that this guy – Gavin – was only staying with her two or three nights a week, but she said she'd told him that he either moved in with her or not to bother coming back. He moved in and so she didn't feel it was right that I would be giving her money when she was living with another man.

During that time, I met a girl called Rachel and we started seeing each other, but the relationship didn't last. However, Rachel had fallen pregnant during the time we were together and gave me my son, Saul. I missed his birth because I was racing across London at short notice to be there after Rachel had gone into labour and I needed to get to Croydon in torrential rain.

By the time I got there, she'd given birth about four minutes before. We drifted apart, despite giving it a go after Saul was born, but it just wasn't right for either of us and we amicably parted.

I don't think Ally was ever completely happy with Gavin and then she became ill on New Year's Day and went into hospital. I went along to see her and check in on how she was doing. She was being treated by the NHS, but I could sense there was urgency in the situation, so I said I was going to get her out of there.

She said, "No Silk – you'll end up spending all your money if you do that."

I said, "Who gives a fuck? How long have you known me? How much do I care about money? I came into the world without a penny, and I'll leave the same way, so who cares?"

I arranged for her to be transferred to the Wellington Hospital in St John's Wood immediately and, as it turns out, they operated on her the night of her arrival. She'd had a cyst that had burst and was poisoning her blood and the doctor told me that if she'd had surgery even 24 hours later than she had, she'd have died.

Tragically, while they were treating her they discovered she also had stage four cancer and told her she had six months to live.

I spoke with Ally and told her I would do everything I could to find alternative treatment. She argued that I was wasting my money and that it would leave me penniless, but she was the mother of my daughter, I'd loved her with all my heart and still did, so there was no question of me not doing everything I could for her.

We had a bit of a fight about it, and I said that if she didn't let me pay for whatever treatment I could find, I would walk away from her and never speak to her again – and I sort of meant it. She said, "You're serious, aren't you?" and I told her I was. So she reluctantly accepted my help.

Around this time, I used to have a birthday party every year in my garden with up to 400 people there.

I'd always have entertainers and a stage, and sometimes my old mate Bobby Davro might do a 20-minute comedy set, or Shalamar or similar providing the music depending on who was available.

Les (Billy Ocean) did a set one time with all his band and backing singers, but he wouldn't charge me a penny for his own appearance.

"Pay the band and backing singers if you want, but I don't want any money off you."

That's how he is.

Another time, I hired a function room at a hotel in London for Ally's birthday.

Her cancer treatment was full-on, and she had wires and tubes everywhere, but I was determined to give her a night she wouldn't forget, and she loved it.

We had a DJ, singers, great food but when it got to 11pm, I went on stage and said, "I'd like to thank everyone for coming and Ally, I hope you've enjoyed it."

She said she had loved it.

"That isn't quite it," I said. "We both love the band Tavares, but they're obviously based in the States, so I tried to find a tribute band who sounded like them and looked like them, but I couldn't. So, without further ado, please welcome to the stage, the one, the only, Tavares Brothers."

They came out from the back in their white suits and Ally just burst out crying. She got up on stage, hugged them, sang a song with them — badly! — and they did a 40-minute set. It was fantastic. We had got really close to the brothers and Butch would stay with us from time to time.

They had travelled from all over the USA to be at the party and they would only let me pay their air fare — that's all they wanted.

At the end of the evening, Ally came over to me and said, "You know what, Silk? No matter how long I live or what happens to me, I'll never ever forget this night."

We looked at each other and she said she loved me, and I told her I loved her. We were actually separated at the time but I knew she would end up back with me.

Ally had treatment in Israel and all around the world, and instead of lasting six months she lasted another two-and-a-half years. I'd told her in the past that if she ever wanted to come home and come back and live at the house we'd shared, she only had to say.

She asked me if that would still be the case if I was living with somebody else. I said they would just have to understand, and if they didn't, then they would have to leave. Ally was the love of my life, and I would never turn my back on her.

I remember after one operation she had 104 stitches and was back at her house with her aunt looking after her. She looked at me and said, "Silk, can I come home?"

I said, "As soon as you're fit enough, yes."

She told me she would be ready in two days, and I told her that was impossible because she had tubes and wires coming out of everywhere, but she said she needed to get away from her old place and – I don't know how – she managed to get herself ready and came home two days later and spent the last year of her life with me.

The treatment kept her going, but there was never going to be a miraculous cure. I knew I would lose her to cancer in the end, and when the day came in February 2016, I was utterly heartbroken, but took a lot of comfort from the extra time we'd had together as a family.

Ally had been in a coma for four days towards the end. On the second day she went to scratch her nose and I scratched it for her, but there was no response when I spoke to her. The day before she died, on the third day of her coma, I leaned in to her and whispered, "Al, I love you so much…" and she just whispered, "I love you too, Silk." For a moment, I thought we were getting her back, but after that, there was no response. I never left her side, except to go back home for a shower at 6am, walk and feed the dogs and return to hospital for around 11am and remain there before repeating the process at 4pm and returning to spend the night by her side. I wasn't sleeping at all, but I needed to be there as much as I could.

Keenia – who Ally and I always called Bubbles – was there as much as she could be and on this particular day, she told her mum she would be back in the evening as she had some stuff to do. When she came back, she told Ally she had been in the recording studio and had recorded a song for her – it was Adele's 'Make You Feel My Love' and she played it to her on her phone.

Halfway through, Ally said, "Bubs, that's beautiful." Those were the last words she ever spoke, and she died the next day. Her breathing changed, Keenia gave her a big kiss, as I did, and shortly after she took her last breath. I can't hear that song any more without breaking down.

My one regret is that I asked Ally if she would remarry me, and she said yes without hesitation. I told her we needed to get her well so we could enjoy it properly, but she never did, and I should have taken a rabbi to the hospital and got married there. She asked to have the name Silkman on her headstone, which she has – but I should have got married again when I still had the chance.

By that time, emotionally and professionally, I was in bits.

I was almost bankrupt and had £30,000 remaining in the bank with a bill of £110,000 to pay. I'd paid out more than £1 million in medical care – all of which I was more than happy to do for the extra time me and Keenia got with Ally, and it was worth every single penny. But I was in trouble.

A close friend learned of my situation and decided he wasn't going to stand by and watch me lose even more than I already had. I'd done a lot of business with him over the years, we'd always got on really well, but what he did was off the charts and something I will never forget. The name of the man in question will remain anonymous, but he is mentioned somewhere in this book.

He paid £100,000 into my bank account with one caveat – that I never paid it back. As I say, I am not going to name who it was – though his name is well known throughout football – because it would embarrass him. He knew what I'd paid out for Ally and why, and just wanted to help me back on my feet. He was there when I needed it most. You know who you are.

That was in 2016 and even though I found it hard to get going again, I woke up one morning and a thought flashed through my mind about how angry Ally would be if she could see me fretting and not being strong.

Gradually, I started to find my feet again and once I was back in the game, I never really looked back again. I believe Ally is watching me from up above and making sure I'm okay, and also believe we'll be together again some day.

At one stage, I represented 27 players, 24 of which were in the Premier League, but in recent years I've focused more on brokering deals than anything else. I still had a good name in football, have great contacts and a lot of trust, so that felt the best way for me to go.

I still work with the agents of Gabriel Martinelli at Arsenal, Tomas Soucek and Lucas Paqueta at West Ham, and with no bullshit, I believe I am the best football negotiator in this country by light years, because I get the best deals coming in and the best deals going out.

There are too many directors of football who get their mates involved to get a payment and they don't care what the club has to pay. I work alone and never use anyone in my deals.

If I'm working for a club, they are my sole focus and not whether I can make myself and others money at their cost.

That's just the way it is and that's how I work, and I'd put myself up against anyone when it comes to getting the best deal. Pini Zahavi says I should negotiate between Israel and Palestine as he's convinced I'd find a peaceful solution to the ongoing conflict! If only that were true…

Chapter 18

THE SHOW MUST GO ON

A colleague of mine once commented that he'd never met anyone with the connections in show business that I had or knew of anyone who knew as many people as I did. He said, "I travel all over the world and have met a lot of people, but wherever I go, your name seems to crop up!"

I was at the London Palladium for Dionne Warwick's farewell tour and was stood by her dressing room when a friend said, "Surely you don't know Dionne Warwick as well?"

I said, "Let me show you something."

So I went into the doorway and Dionne was surrounded by people chatting to her, so I just shouted, "Oi! Are you going to leave me out here or are you going to talk to me?"

She looked around and said, "Silky! How are you?"

This guy who had asked if I knew her said, "I don't fucking believe it. Is there anyone you don't know?"

Dionne said, "Get out of the way folks, I need to see my special man."

She was too exhausted to get up, so I went over, gave her a hug and she said that I should have let her know I was in the audience because she would have given me a mention between songs.

But everything went up a notch when I became friends – and eventually business partners – with David Gest.

David, the former husband of Liza Minnelli, was a producer and entertainment impresario who had worked closely with Michael Jackson and had a very successful PR company in New York. I met him through a friend of mine, Mark Aaron, who I'd worked with as a tour promoter for acts like Gwen Dickey of Rose Royce fame, Alexander O'Neal, and some other top-name soul acts.

David knew Michael Jackson very well and he told me many stories about him, and he insists there was no way on Earth that Michael was anything like the way he has been portrayed since his death – far from it. He insists Jackson had many, many girlfriends – or occasional acquaintances – that only those closest to him were aware of it.

He told me he was a lunatic for sex and that the accusations that were filed against him were so far away from what he really was. He just loved women – that's what David Gest told me, and he knew Michael for many years. I never met him, so I can only go on what others told me.

Gwen got me some back-stage passes for one of her shows and David Gest was there and he came over and asked if I was meant to be back stage. I told him I was a friend of Gwen, and he asked my name and I said "Silky". He said that was a great name, it was good to meet me, and he hoped we'd meet again.

At the end of the night, he said we should swap numbers and that I should go and see one of the shows he was promoting.

So we did, he texted me a few days later and told me we had a mutual friend that had been singing my praises – a Newcastle United player – and that we should meet up for a coffee. A few days later, we had that coffee and chatted, and he said maybe I could link up with him and put a few of my artists on one of his shows. I told him that sounded good. I organised some acts to appear on his bill and it went well, and afterwards David asked if I wanted to be a partner with him.

THE SHOW MUST GO ON

I said I would if I could remain a silent partner, because at the time I didn't want that to be public knowledge as I had enough to deal with being a football agent.

David and I became good friends, and he was devastated when Ally died, but he said he wouldn't be at the funeral because he was superstitious and thought he would jinx himself – instead, he would come around and see me a few days after.

He was suffering with a terrible cold at the time and told me he was due to go on *Celebrity Big Brother*, but I said, "Why are you doing that? You're too ill."

He said he knew he was, but he was getting well paid and that some of the money was going to charitable causes, plus he didn't want to let anyone down.

So, he went on and was bedridden for most of the time he was in the *Big Brother* house with what must have been a severe case of flu but was involved – albeit indirectly – in one of the most infamous moments in the show's history.

Angie Bowie was also on the show, and she confided with fellow housemate Tiffany Pollard – an excitable American TV presenter – that 'David had died'. She meant her ex-husband David Bowie, who had just passed away, but Tiffany lost the plot because she thought David Gest had died and the production crew were trying to keep it quiet.

It ended with the housemates rushing to the bedroom

area to check on poor David who was under the covers, sick – but thankfully breathing! He poked his head out and said, "No, I'm still alive!"

David, as it turned out, was forced to leave shortly after due to his ill-health – but it's fair to say he had a sizeable impact without doing anything other than be ill, though everyone loved him when he did manage to get up and about. In fact, he finished fourth overall and there were stories that 30,000 text votes for him had been lost because of a glitch in the voting.

Prior to going into the show, we had organised for a collection of artists to come to the UK on tour and he'd asked me to come up with a name for it. In previous years he had called it The David Gest Soul Tour but wanted something different. Unfortunately, I'm useless with stuff like that so when he came back to me a few weeks later, he asked if I had thought up a new name. I said, "Yes. The David Gest Soul Tour."

He laughed and said that was what we called it all the time and that he'd have a think when he was in the *Celebrity Big Brother* house.

After he departed, he called me up almost straight away and said, "Silks, I've got a name for the tour. It's going to be called 'David Gest Is Not Dead But Alive With Soul'."

It was a brilliant name.

The tour was due to start at the beginning of June,

but because of the delay in naming it officially, we had a race against time to try and get the tickets sold. We had a couple of venues to look at and one was in Bournemouth, so I called him on the day we were due to drive to the south coast, but he didn't answer. I kept trying, texted him and nothing. I did the same the following day with no luck and no reply.

I was out the next night at a music venue, and somebody asked about David and said he should come in with me some time to have a look around and I said I'd ask him – but I was having trouble getting hold of him. He said, "Try him now while you're here." I did, and still nothing. It was odd.

He lived in a room at the Four Seasons Hotel at Canary Wharf, so I called the reception and asked if anyone had seen David. They hadn't, but a girl who worked at the hotel and did a bit of PA work for David told me she thought he might have gone to Leeds for the weekend on business.

David had mentioned Leeds to me, but that didn't explain why he'd missed the trip to Bournemouth or hadn't answered my calls, so I said to the girl, "Look, I need somebody to go and check on him." She had doubts because David had a habit of losing his rag if he was disturbed when he didn't want to be and he had a 'do not disturb' hanger on his door handle.

I said I understood, but an hour later I decided enough

was enough and insisted somebody go and check he was okay. Within an hour I got a call to say they'd found David dead in his suite. It looked like he'd had a shower and collapsed and died after suffering a heart attack and stroke. He'd been dead about four days.

It was a huge shock, and I'd lost a good friend.

But there was a huge complication that I contractually had to deal with. There was a tour still to do with acts who would have to be paid whether they performed or not and that tour, as mentioned before, was called 'David Gest Is Not Dead But Alive With Soul'. I couldn't have made it up if I tried and with only about six weeks before the tour began, I couldn't change the name now.

David's lawyer informed me we couldn't use the tour name, but I was by that point a few weeks away from the tour starting with not a single ticket sold. An associate of mine went to Tennessee to try and convince his lawyers, and after we gave certain assurances that we would pay tribute to David during the tour, they finally agreed we could go ahead with the tour as it was named.

We had a video of David and tributes played at each gig and Freda Payne – who was close to David – hosted the event and I was saved from certain bankruptcy as I just about got my money back.

The Times, Freda Payne, Rose Royce, Peabo Bryson, Deniece Williams and about 12 artists in total all came on the tour – plus Dina Carroll who I'd personally wanted to be part of the tour and hadn't sang for 14 years – and it went well and was a great epitaph to David's life and work.

Another time I worked with Mark Aaron was when I ended up agreeing to manage Mike Tyson in the UK. Mark told me Tyson had no real management as such and was difficult to handle but was looking to come over to the UK on tour. I said I'd love to and got to work immediately. I spoke with a number of venues – mostly hotels – who were all keen to do 'An Audience With' events with Mike.

Mike knew me as Silky, and we had several discussions over the phone, and we got along really well. We had an agreement in place, and he came over to London and I met him at the airport. He said to me, "I know another Silky but you're nothing like the one I know."

I asked him how I was different, and he said, "Well, firstly, he's about six feet two, secondly, he is black, and thirdly, he's the biggest drug dealer in New York City."

I agreed we were two different Silkys!

We put him up at the Marriott in Waltham Abbey and he signed a few papers to say I'd be representing him whenever he came to England, book him for shows and stuff like that. He'd brought over a few minders with him and on the morning he was due to fly home, I went to his hotel to say goodbye and one of his minders met me in reception and said, "Silks, I wouldn't bother with him today – he's in a vile mood."

I said, "Nah, I'll be fine," but he pleaded with me not to.

I walked across the reception and saw him walking towards with me with a limping walk, with a hoodie over his head and almost walking along the wall.

I stood in his way and he didn't have a clue who I was because he could only see my feet. The minders were shaking their head, but he just took his hood off, looked at me and said, "Silky, my brother" and gave me a hug and kiss!

We sat down, had a coffee and he was fantastic. As we were all leaving, the minder who had warned me when I'd arrived said "I don't know how you did that. He's completely flipped around because he was so angry before you came."

We just hit it off and it's such a shame I can't get him a visa because of one or two problems he had back home, and I have tried three or four times. He'd sell out venues for several thousand people no problem today, so it's frustrating.

I also did some management in the music business. Another guy I'd been promoting for many years asked if I would become his manager – Alexander O'Neal. I met him again through Mark Aaron and got on really well with him.

THE SHOW MUST GO ON

Alex had been struggling for several years for one reason or another, and nobody would take him on. But I did and I told him, "Alex, I'm going to get you back to where you should be" – and we did exactly that. He worked hard to get back to where he needed to be and a while later, he did a show at the Indigo At The 02 Arena in front of 2,500 fans.

During his set, instead of talking between songs as he usually did, he just sang, and the place was going mental. Then, he paused the show and said, "There is one person that I need to thank for being back here today – without him, I don't know where I'd be at this moment. I owe him everything."

I was thinking, "Who the fuck is he on about?"

Then he said, "Silky, step up on the stage."

Shit!

I went up and he said, "Silky, thank you for everything. And they tell me you can sing a bit, too? Well I hope it's true."

With that, he gave me a mic and left me standing on my own on the stage in front of 2,500 people. I knew only one of his songs really well all the way through – 'If You Were Here Tonight' – and so I asked the band leader what they were about to play, and he said, 'If You Were Here Tonight'.

My luck was in. I started singing and Alex came on after a minute or two and we finished the song together.

At the end, he gave me a hug and I whispered, "Ever do that again and I'll fucking kill you!" What an experience, though.

I did another tour with Alex and his farewell tour in 2024. He got back on track just in time because he was heading towards a bad place, but he's calmed down and is back to the real Alexander O'Neal, and I'm proud to call him a good friend.

During the farewell tour, I sort of got my own back on him at the Royal Albert Hall of all places!

He was doing a show in front of a packed audience and halfway through the set, I came on stage with his partner of 35 years, Cynthia Alexander.

She didn't know what was going on, but Alex did and when we got to him, he asked her if she would be his wife – she was ecstatic, and the crowd went mad when she said yes.

I'd organised for an American minister to join us on stage and he married them, right there and then.

As the crowd clapped and applauded, Alex said into my ear, "You've got to sing 'If You Were Here Tonight'," but I said, "Sorry Alex, I've got to meet someone now, I can't do it," and exited stage left!

I thought, 'No chance! Me sing at a packed Royal Albert Hall in front of 5,000 people? Not happening!'

Alex later asked who I had to go and see so urgently, and I told him, "No-one!"

I still love doing the soul tours to this day, but you have to make sure you get the business and passion balanced or it can all go wrong. It's a fantastic business to be in, but very hard work, yet hugely enjoyable.

The problem I have is that I've met too many people and I have probably forgotten more than I remember. Some were just at showbiz parties, others I might have helped them in their careers somehow or whatever, so it can be embarrassing when people come up to me and I either can't place them or have forgotten what I did to help them.

I count myself lucky that I have been able to have a dual existence between football and the entertainment world.

I had a good playing career – maybe not what it could have been, but I am grateful that I had the chance – and I got to sing a lot.

I often wonder if that misunderstanding with Mickie Most had never happened, whether I would have gone on to be a successful artist. But again, I was lucky to even have that opportunity, and I can always ask the question, 'what if?'

I've had a great life and done most of the things I wanted to at one level or another. I'm in my 73rd year on this planet, still work in football at a high level and I'm still bringing some fantastic acts to this country on the soul tours.

I have Keenia, my daughter; I have my son Saul, and my grandson Eran. I feel fit as a fiddle.

Honestly, what more could I ask for?

Acknowledgements

Thanking all the people who have helped me along the way and made me the person I am today is nigh on impossible – where do you even begin! There will be people who mean a lot to me that won't be included in the names here, but if that's the case, I'll put that right in the reprints of this book as I'm expecting a few phone calls!

I'll begin at the beginning with my parents who taught me many things and instilled the values in me that have served me well all my life. They are: family comes first, work hard and treat others the way you want to be treated and – and this is mostly directed at my mum – don't take any shit from anyone.

Thanks, of course, to my daughter Keenia, son Saul and grandson Eran, and to Ally.

People from the football world are too numerous to mention, but I can't not include Terry Venables who was such a big part of my life, on and off the football pitch. 'TV', as I called him, played beautiful football, was an innovator ahead of his time, and was a talented man away from the game, as a writer and singer and I learned so much from him as well as discovering the world of show business and all the glitz and glamour that went with it.

I'd also like to thank my ghostwriter, David Clayton, for his patience and understanding as one deadline after another passed, and also my publishers Reach for their faith in bringing my story to print.